1er octobre 2002

À Joanie &
Simon...
en prévision de notre
expérience américaine
qui arrive à grands pas!

Janique &
Martin
xxx

Mon Premier Larousse d'Anglais

ILLUSTRATIONS

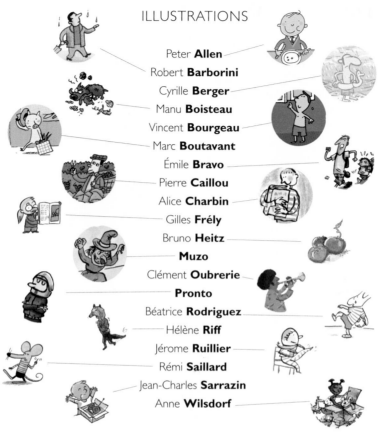

Peter **Allen**

Robert **Barborini**

Cyrille **Berger**

Manu **Boisteau**

Vincent **Bourgeau**

Marc **Boutavant**

Émile **Bravo**

Pierre **Caillou**

Alice **Charbin**

Gilles **Frély**

Bruno **Heitz**

Muzo

Clément **Oubrerie**

Pronto

Béatrice **Rodriguez**

Hélène **Riff**

Jérome **Ruillier**

Rémi **Saillard**

Jean-Charles **Sarrazin**

Anne **Wilsdorf**

Illustration de couverture:
Émile **Bravo**

Direction artistique, conception graphique & réalisation:
F. Houssin & C. Ramadier pour **DOUBLE**
Direction éditoriale: Françoise **Vibert-Guigue**
Édition: Anne **Delcourt**
Conseil: Isabelle **Courvoisier** et Ursula **Payne**, professeurs d'anglais
Direction de la publication: Dominique **Korach**
Fabrication: Jacques **Lannoy**

© Larousse / VUEF 2001 • 21, rue du Montparnasse - 75006 Paris
ISBN 2-03-553017-2 • Imprimé en Espagne par GRAFICAS ESTELLA • Photogravure: OFFSET ESSONNE
Dépôt légal: septembre 2001 • N° de projet: 10081189 (I)
Conforme à la loi n° 49956 du 16 juillet 1949 sur les publications destinées à la jeunesse.

❶ 1000 mots regroupés par thèmes

Pour être plus efficace qu'un dictionnaire classique, *Mon Premier Larousse d'Anglais* est organisé par thèmes, chacun avec sa couleur: **la famille, la maison, la nourriture, l'école, les vacances**...

Des thèmes familiers aux enfants, qui apprennent ainsi l'anglais comme ils ont appris à parler.

Chaque mot qu'ils découvrent mène à d'autres: brother (frère) à sister (sœur), laugh (rire) à cry (pleurer), etc...

Pour faciliter ce travail d'association entre les mots, certains mots sont présentés dans des encadrés de couleur.

❷ Des mots pour donner tout de suite envie de parler

Les 1000 mots de *Mon Premier Larousse d'Anglais* ont été soigneusement sélectionnés dans l'univers des enfants. Ils forment un **vocabulaire** de base suffisamment **riche** et **varié** pour permettre aux enfants de commencer à parler en anglais.

friend
ami, copain
Frances and Philip
are friends.

bother
ennuyer, embêter
"Stop
bothering me!"

Et puisqu'on apprend aussi en s'amusant, on a placé en tête de chaque page un petit **jeu de memory**.

❸ La grammaire

À la fin du livre quelques tableaux très simples donnent les règles de grammaire indispensables pour bien utiliser les **noms**, les **verbes**, les **adjectifs** et les **expressions** du dictionnaire.

❹ Deux index

Un index **anglais - français** et un index **français - anglais** permettent de retrouver immédiatement le mot que l'on cherche.

Contents, Sommaire

Hello!, Bonjour! → 6

Useful words, Des mots utiles → 8

Numbers, Les chiffres → 10

Colours and shapes, Les couleurs et les formes → 11

Days and months, Des jours et des mois → 12

Who am I?, Qui suis-je? → 14

My family, Ma famille → 16

The body, Le corps → 18

The five senses, Les cinq sens → 20

Health, La santé → 22

At the doctor's, Chez le docteur → 23

On the move, En mouvement → 24

Feelings, Les sentiments → 26

Thinking, Penser → 30

Speaking, Parler → 32

A child's day, La journée d'un enfant → 34

Clothes, Les vêtements → 36

Meals, Les repas → 38

Breakfast, Le petit déjeuner → 39

Food, La nourriture → 40

Sweet things, Desserts et sucreries → 42

Drinks, Les boissons → 43

Vegetables, Les légumes → 44

Fruit, Les fruits → 45

At home, À la maison → 46

The sitting room, Le salon → 48

The bedroom, La chambre → 50

The bathroom, La salle de bains → 51

The kitchen, La cuisine → 52

The garden, Le jardin → 53

Little things, Les petits objets → 54

Action!, Action! → 56

Getting on with people, S'entendre avec les autres → 60

Expressions, Expressions → 61

In my opinion, À mon avis → 62

Opposites, Les contraires → 65

At school, À l'école → 68

Sport, Les sports → 72

Hobbies, Les loisirs → 74

Music!, Musique! → 77

Jobs, Les métiers → 78

Shopping, Les courses → 80

In town, En ville → 82

On the road, Sur la route → 84

Transport, Les transports → 86

Travelling, En voyage → 88

Winter sports, Les sports d'hiver → 89

At the seaside, Au bord de la mer → 90

In the country, À la campagne → 92

On the farm, À la ferme → 94

At the zoo, Au zoo → 96

The weather, Le temps qu'il fait → 98

The Universe, L'Univers → 100

Let's celebrate!, Faisons la fête! → 101

Time, Le temps qui passe → 102

Here and there, Ici et là → 106

From the beginning to the end, Du début jusqu'à la fin → 109

Quantities, Les quantités → 110

A little grammar, un peu de grammaire → 112

Index, English-French → 120

French-English → 133

Retrouve les mots anglais qui correspondent à ces silhouettes.

Hello !
Bonjour !

darling
chéri, chérie

"Darling, I love you!"

dear
cher, chère

"Come here, dear child!"

excuse me
excusez-moi, pardon

"Excuse me, Miss..."

How are you?
Comment ça va?

"How are you,
Mr Wolf?"
"Very well, thank you."

Mr, Mrs
Monsieur, Madame

This is Mr and Mrs
Smith.

Please!

please
s'il te plaît, s'il vous plaît

See you
soon!

see you soon
à bientôt

See you
tomorrow!

see you
tomorrow
à demain

Sorry!

sorry
pardon, désolé

6

thank you
merci
"Thank you, dear!"

this is...
voici
"This is Andy."

welcome
bienvenue
"Welcome to the party!"

hello
bonjour, salut
"Hello, Mr Jones!"

good morning
bonjour (le matin)
"Good morning, Fox!"

good afternoon
bonjour (l'après-midi)
"Good afternoon, Fox!"

good evening
bonsoir
"Good evening, Fox!"

goodnight
bonne nuit
"Goodnight, Mum!"

goodbye
au revoir
"Goodbye, Becky!"

Useful words

Des mots utiles

and

et

Cedric and Fred.

even

même

Even on holidays,
Ivan is sad.

into

dans

Minnie is jumping
into the box.

because

parce que

Ben is in bed
because he is ill.

for

pour

"It is for you!"

like

comme

Larry is crying
like a baby.

but

mais

Small but strong!

if

si

"If you go, I go!"

not

ne pas

"I am not going
in there!"

only
seulement
"Only one, please!"

perhaps
peut-être
Perhaps it will rain,
perhaps not.

with
avec
Cedric with Fred.

or
ou
"Chocolate
or vanilla?"

very
très
The teacher
is very angry.

without
sans
Cedric without Fred.

yes
oui

no
non

from
de
Pedro comes
from Mexico.

to
à, au
The baby
is going
to the park.

Retrouve les mots anglais qui correspondent à ces silhouettes.

Numbers

Les nombres

0 zero	1 one	2 two	3 three	4 four
5 five	6 six	7 seven	8 eight	9 nine
10 ten	11 eleven	12 twelve	13 thirteen	14 fourteen
15 fifteen	16 sixteen	17 seventeen	18 eighteen	19 nineteen
20 twenty	30 thirty	40 fourty	50 fifty	60 sixty
70 seventy	80 eighty	90 ninety	100 one hundred	1000 one thousand

first   second   third   fourth   fifth   sixth   seventh   eighth   ninth   tenth

Colours and shapes

Les couleurs et les formes

Retrouve les mots anglais qui correspondent à ces silhouettes.

red

blue

yellow

pink

brown

grey

orange

green

purple

white

black

circle
cercle

—

round
rond

—

square
carré

rectangle
rectangle

—

diamond
losange

—

triangle
triangle

11

Retrouve
les mots anglais
qui correspondent
à ces silhouettes.

Days and months

Des jours et des mois

day
jour
What day is it?

month
mois
There are twelve
months in a year.

time
heure, temps
"What time is it,
please?"

timetable
emploi du temps
The timetable
of the week.

watch
montre
A watch tells the time.

weekend
week-end
Wendy likes
weekends.

one o'clock — two o'clock

three o'clock — four o'clock

five o'clock — six o'clock

seven o'clock — eight o'clock

nine o'clock — ten o'clock

eleven o'clock — twelve o'clock

five past one — five to one

a quarter past one — half past one

the time
l'heure

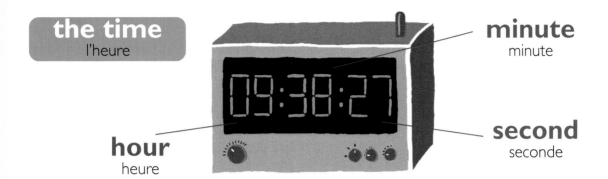

minute
minute

second
seconde

hour
heure

a week
une semaine

Monday	**Tuesday**	**Wednesday**	**Thursday**	**Friday**	**Saturday**	**Sunday**
lundi	mardi	mercredi	jeudi	vendredi	samedi	dimanche

a year
un an, une année

January	**February**	**March**	**April**	**May**	**June**
janvier	février	mars	avril	mai	juin

July	**August**	**September**	**October**	**November**	**December**
juillet	août	septembre	octobre	novembre	décembre

Who am I?

Qui suis-je?

adult
adulte
Andy
is an adult.

baby
bébé
Benny is a baby.

boy
garçon
Bob
is a boy.

child/children
enfant/enfants
Charles is a child.
Charlene is a child.
Charles and Charlene
are children.

fat
gros, grosse
Francis is fat.

girl
fille
Gloria
is a girl.

man/men
homme/hommes
Mark is a man.
Mike is a man.
Mark and Mike
are men.

name
nom
"My name is Nadia."

people
gens
People at a party.

person
personne
Peter is a person.
Garfield is an animal.

small
petit, petite
The baby is small.

strong
fort, forte
Stan is strong.

tall
grand, grande
Tony is tall.

thin
mince
Ruth is thin.

woman/women
femme/femmes
Wendy is a woman.
Winnie is a woman.
Wendy and Winnie
are women.

young
jeune
Two young children.

old
vieux, vieille
Fred's grandfather
is old.

how old
quel âge

How old
are you?

I am three
years old.

I am ... years old.
J'ai ... ans.

My family

Ma famille

my grandparents
mes grands-parents

my grandfather
mon grand-père

my grandmother
ma grand-mère

my grandfather
mon grand-père

my grandmother
ma grand-mère

my parents
mes parents

my mother
ma mère

my father
mon père

my aunt
ma tante

my uncle
mon oncle

my brother
mon frère

me
moi

my sister
ma sœur

my cousins
mes cousins

child/children
enfant/enfants
Tom and Emma Smith
have two children.

divorced
divorcé, divorcée
Dina's parents
are divorced.

get married
se marier
Gus and Mary
are getting married.

husband
mari
Aunt Jane with
her husband Jack.

pregnant
enceinte
Peggy is pregnant.

wife/wives
femme/femmes
Uncle Jack
with his wife Jane.

daddy, dad
papa
Daddy and David.

---

mummy, mum
maman
David and Mummy.

---

daughter son
fille - fils
Eve and Adam Jones
have a daughter
and a son.

The body

Le corps

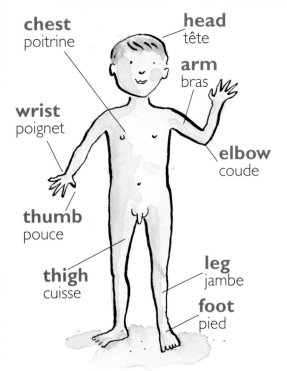

chest
poitrine

head
tête

arm
bras

wrist
poignet

elbow
coude

thumb
pouce

thigh
cuisse

leg
jambe

foot
pied

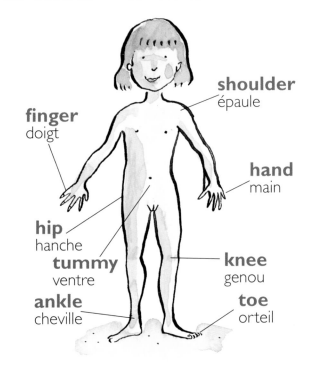

shoulder
épaule

finger
doigt

hand
main

hip
hanche

tummy
ventre

knee
genou

ankle
cheville

toe
orteil

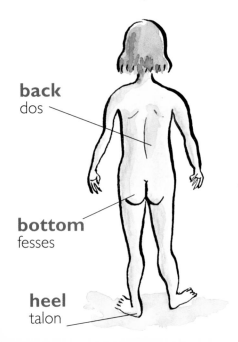

back
dos

bottom
fesses

heel
talon

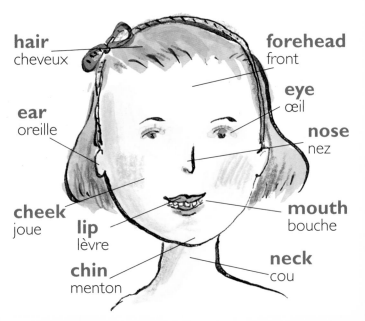

hair
cheveux

forehead
front

eye
œil

ear
oreille

nose
nez

cheek
joue

lip
lèvre

mouth
bouche

chin
menton

neck
cou

18

blood
sang
"Oh, no! There is blood on my knee!"

tongue
langue
"Look at my tongue!"

tooth/teeth
dent/dents
The baby has one tooth.

face
visage
Wayne is washing his face.

nail
ongle
Ned has long nails.

short hair
cheveux courts

long hair
cheveux longs

straight hair
cheveux raides

curly hair
cheveux frisés, bouclés

Retrouve les mots anglais qui correspondent à ces silhouettes.

The five senses

Les cinq sens

hard

dur, dure

This is hard!

—

hear

entendre

Hilda can hear the sea.

listen (to)

écouter

"Listen to me!"

—

look (at)

regarder

"Look at the boat!"

noise

bruit

"Stop that noise, please!"

—

noisy

bruyant, bruyante

Children are noisy!

ouch!

aïe !

atishoo!

atchoum !

shh!

chut!

ha ha!

hi hi!

20

see
voir
"Can you see
the boat?"

—

smell
sentir
The cake smells
delicious.

—

soft
doux, douce
This is soft.

taste
goûter ; avoir du goût
The cake tastes
delicious.

—

touch
toucher
"Don't touch
the bread!"

—

watch
observer, regarder
Paul is watching
a bird.

cold
froid, froide
Tony is cold.

—

warm
chaud, chaude
Wendy is warm.

—

hot
trop chaud(e), brûlant(e)
Harry is hot.

Retrouve
les mots anglais
qui correspondent
à ces silhouettes.

Health

La santé

cold

rhume

Charles has a cold.

healthy

en bonne santé

Harry is healthy.

ill

malade

Iris is ill.

dentist

dentiste

Debbie at the dentist's.

hospital

hôpital

The helicopter is
on the hospital.

medicine

médicament

Iris needs
a medicine.

doctor

médecin

Dennis at the doctor's.

Ouch!

hurt

avoir mal ; (se) faire mal

"My knee hurts!"

feel sick

avoir mal au cœur

Simon feels sick.

Retrouve
les mots anglais
qui correspondent
à ces silhouettes.

At the doctor's

Chez le docteur

squeeze
presser

weigh
peser

check
vérifier

swallow
avaler

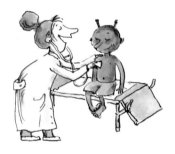

listen
écouter

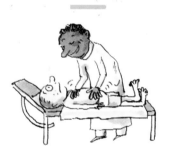

feel
sentir, palper

measure
mesurer

examine
examiner

cough
tousser

Retrouve les mots anglais qui correspondent à ces silhouettes.

On the move

En mouvement

climb
grimper
Cliff is climbing.

jump
sauter
The cat is jumping.

move
bouger
"Don't move!"

fall
tomber
The cat is falling.

leave
quitter, partir de
The children are leaving school.

run
courir
Ron is running.

go
aller
"We are going to the beach!"

lie
être allongé
Linda is lying on the beach.

sit
être assis
Sidney is sitting on a chair.

24

sit down
s'asseoir
Samia is sitting down.

—

walk
marcher
The baby walks!

walk
promenade
A walk in the woods…

stand up
se lever
"Stand up, please!"

—

stay
rester
Stan is staying
in bed.

Come here!

Come down, Kitty!

come (here)
venir

—

come down
descendre

—

Come back, Cathy!

Come in, Kitty!

come back
revenir

come in
entrer

Feelings

Les sentiments

be afraid
avoir peur
Alfred is afraid.

be ashamed
avoir honte
Alan is ashamed.

brave
courageux
Betty is brave.

angry
en colère
Andy is angry !

be bored
s'ennuyer
Bob is bored.

clever
malin, intelligent
This cat is clever!

like
bien aimer
Lewis likes his toy.

love
aimer
Lucy loves Peter.

hate
détester
Harriet hates spinach.

disappointed
déçu, déçue
The princess is
disappointed!

frightened
effrayé(e)
Fiona is frightened.

lazy
paresseux, paresseuse
"Wake up, lazy boy!"

excited
excité(e), agité(e)
The children
are excited!

hope
espérer
Emily hopes the rain
will stop.

laugh
rire
Leo and Lenny
love laughing.

feel
sentir ; se sentir
Felix feels lazy.

kind
gentil, gentille
The baker is kind.

cry
pleurer
Chris is crying.

miss
manquer
Chris misses his cat.

pleased
content, contente
Paula is pleased.

quiet
calme, tranquille
Tom and Ben
are quiet.

mood
humeur
Max is in a bad mood.
Molly is in a good
mood.

prefer
préférer
Lucy likes chocolate.
Penny prefers vanilla.

shy
timide
Shirley is shy.

happy
heureux
Hanna
is happy.

unhappy
malheureux
Ursula
is unhappy.

glad
content ; heureux
Glenda is glad.

sad
triste
Sam is sad.

smile
sourire
Simon is smiling.

surprised
étonné, étonnée
Sue is surprised:
Cecilia can swim!

worry
s'inquiéter
Mummy is worried:
Cecilia is late!

strict
sévère
Sarah's father
is strict.

temper
caractère
Tess is bad-tempered !

polite
poli, polie
Polly is polite.

stupid
stupide
This cat is stupid.

want
vouloir
The cat wants milk.

rude
impoli, impolie
Richard is rude.

29

Thinking

Penser

forget
oublier
"Don't forget your scarf!"

know
savoir ; connaître
"I know that story!"

remember
se souvenir de
Rita remembers Christmas.

guess
deviner
"Guess what is in my hand!"

mistake
erreur
A little mistake?

understand
comprendre
"I don't understand."

idea
idée
"I have an idea!"

problem
problème
Mr Wolf has a problem.

wonder
se demander
William wonders where his sweets are.

believe
croire

true
vrai

lie
mensonge

sure
sûr

of course
bien sûr

Retrouve
les mots anglais
qui correspondent
à ces silhouettes.

Speaking
Parler

answer
réponse ; répondre
Three children
know the answer.

ask
demander
Thomas asks
a question.

call
appeler
Mummy
is calling Colin.

question
question
"That's a good
question!"

say
dire
"Say yes, please!"

secret
secret
Simon and Sarah
have a secret.

shout
crier
The children
are shouting.

I speak
English.

speak
parler

talk
discuter, parler
Ted and Tony
are talking in bed.

tell
dire, raconter
Dad is telling
Tess a story.

tell off
gronder
Mummy is telling off
Tim and Tom.

word
mot
"Shh!
Not a word!"

what
que, quoi
"What is this?"

where
où
"Where is my
schoolbag?"

who
qui
"Who is there?"

Why not?

No!

why
pourquoi

when
quand
"When are we going
to eat, Mummy?"

how
comment
"How does it work?"

33

Retrouve
les mots anglais
qui correspondent
à ces silhouettes.

A child's day

La journée d'un enfant

Tom wakes up.
Tom se réveille.

Tom gets up.
Tom se lève.

He **eats** his breakfast.
Il mange son petit déjeuner.

Then, he **gets dressed**.
Puis il s'habille.

He **goes** to school.
Il va à l'école.

He **works**
in the classroom.
Il travaille dans la classe.

He **has lunch**.
Il déjeune.

In the afternoon,
he is very **busy**.
L'après-midi, il est très occupé.

Tom has a snack.
Tom prend son goûter.

School is over.
L'école est finie.

Tom has fun
with his dog.
Tom s'amuse avec son chien.

He has a bath.
Il prend son bain.

He has dinner with his mum and dad.
Il dîne avec son papa et sa maman.

He is tired. He goes to bed.
Il est fatigué. Il se couche.

Tom is asleep. Sleep well, Tom!
Tom dort. Dors bien, Tom !

Retrouve
les mots anglais
qui correspondent
à ces silhouettes.

Clothes

Les vêtements

T-shirt
tee-shirt

sock
chaussette

scarf
écharpe ;
foulard

knickers
culotte

nightdress
chemise de nuit

tights
collant

raincoat
imperméable

shirt
chemise

coat
manteau

cap
casquette

skirt
jupe

belt
ceinture

jacket
blouson

blouse
chemisier

cardigan
gilet

boot
botte

shoe
chaussure

trousers
pantalon

dungarees
salopette

dress
robe
A yellow dress.

___

hat
chapeau
A pink hat.

___

jeans
jeans
Jerry loves his jeans.

___

jumper
pull
A green jumper and a red jumper.

pyjamas
pyjama
Yellow pyjamas.

trainers
baskets, tennis
Rex likes trainers.

naked
nu
Penny is naked.

get dressed
s'habiller
Penny is getting dressed.

put on
mettre
Penny is putting on her trousers.

take off
enlever
Penny is taking off her trousers.

wear
porter
Penny is wearing a skirt.

dressed
habillé
Penny is dressed.

Retrouve
les mots anglais
qui correspondent
à ces silhouettes.

Meals

Les repas

cook
cuisiner ; cuire
Kate learns to cook.

eat
manger
Gareth is eating
grapes.

be thirsty
avoir soif
Thelma is thirsty.

delicious
délicieux, délicieuse
"Yummy!
It's delicious!"

meal
repas
A good meal.

lunch
déjeuner
"Lunch is ready!"

drink
boire
They are drinking.

breakfast
petit déjeuner
Brendan is having
breakfast.

dinner
dîner
Daddy at dinner.

Retrouve
les mots anglais
qui correspondent
à ces silhouettes.

Breakfast

Le petit déjeuner

bread
pain
Brian loves bread.

YUCK!

coffee
café
Calvin doesn't like
coffee.

jam
confiture
Janet is making jam.

butter
beurre
Bread and butter.

honey
miel
Bees make honey.

milk
lait
Babies drink milk.

cereal
céréales
Cindy is eating cereal
for breakfast.

be hungry
avoir faim
The cat is hungry.

tea
thé
The Queen
is making tea.

Food

La nourriture

beef

bœuf

A good plate of beef.

chips

frites

Charles loves chips.

flour

farine

Bread is made
with flour.

I like cheese!

cheese

fromage

fish/fishes

poisson/poissons

Three fishes
are cooking.

ham

jambon

A ham sandwich.

chicken

poulet

The chicken
is cooking.

salt

sel

A lot of salt!

pepper

poivre

Too much pepper!

hamburger
hamburger
Harry likes
hamburgers.

meat
viande
A butcher
sells meat.

pasta
pâtes
Paul loves pasta.

pizza
pizza
Cheese pizza
or ham pizza?

rice
riz
Rice is nice.

sandwich
sandwich
A big sandwich.

sausage
saucisse
Three sausages.

slice
tranche
"Have a slice of
bread."

egg
œuf
Two eggs.

bacon
bacon
Bacon and eggs.

41

Sweet things

Desserts et sucreries

biscuit
biscuit

Rex wants a biscuit.

custard
crème anglaise

Camilla loves custard.

sugar
sucre

"Sugar is bad for you!"

cake
gâteau

A birthday cake.

ice cream
glace

Iris likes ice cream.

sweet
bonbon

Simon likes sweets.

chocolate
chocolat

Rex wants chocolate.

pie
tarte

"Can I taste your pie?"

yoghurt
yaourt

Yasmina is eating yoghurt.

Drinks

Les boissons

Retrouve les mots anglais qui correspondent à ces silhouettes.

soda

soda

fruit juice

jus de fruit

tea

thé

cocoa
hot chocolate

cacao, chocolat chaud

milk

lait

water

eau

wine

vin

coffee

café

cider

cidre

43

Retrouve
les mots anglais
qui correspondent
à ces silhouettes.

Vegetables

Les légumes

bean

haricot

cabbage

chou

carrot

carotte

cauliflower

chou-fleur

cucumber

concombre

leek

poireau

lettuce

laitue

pea

petit pois

potato

pomme de terre

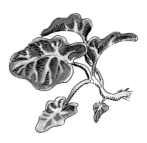

spinach

épinards

tomato

tomate

Retrouve
les mots anglais
qui correspondent
à ces silhouettes.

Fruit

Les fruits

apple
pomme

banana
banane

cherry
cerise

grapes
raisin

lemon
citron

orange
orange

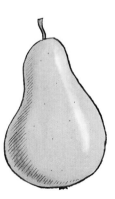

pear
poire

pineapple
ananas

plum
prune

strawberry
fraise

Retrouve
les mots anglais
qui correspondent
à ces silhouettes.

At home

À la maison

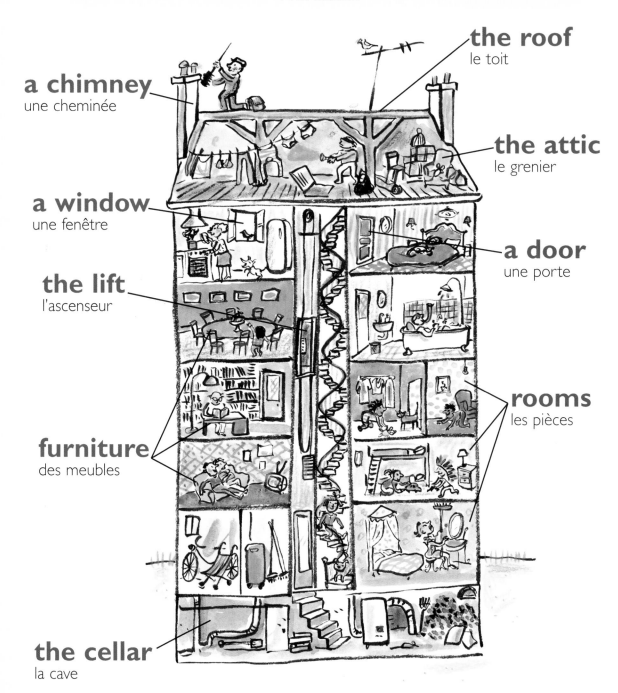

the roof
le toit

a chimney
une cheminée

the attic
le grenier

a window
une fenêtre

a door
une porte

the lift
l'ascenseur

rooms
les pièces

furniture
des meubles

the cellar
la cave

address

adresse

"Here is my address."

key

clé

wall

mur

Willy is building
a wall.

flat

appartement

Fay lives in a flat.

live

vivre ; habiter

Lily lives in Paris.

stairs

escalier

Stella is climbing
the stairs.

house

maison

A big house.

neighbour

voisin, voisine

Nancy and Nina
are neighbours.

downstairs
upstairs

en bas - en haut

Don is going
downstairs. Ursula
is going upstairs.

The sitting room

Le salon

armchair

fauteuil

Grandfather
in his armchair.

comfortable

confortable

The sofa is very
comfortable.

drawer

tiroir

"Open, stupid
drawer!"

bookshelf/
bookshelves

rayonnage/rayonnages

Books on the
bookshelves.

curtain

rideau

Who is behind
the curtain?

fire - fireplace

feu - cheminée

Frank is making
a fire in the fireplace.

carpet

tapis

A magic carpet?

cushion

coussin

A cat on the cushion.

floor

sol ; plancher

A cat on the floor.

lamp
lampe
The lamp is broken.

radio
radio
Ray is listening
to the radio.

television, TV
télévision
Ted is watching
television.

light
lumière
There is a light
in the street.

sofa
canapé
The dog is sitting
on the sofa.

video
video
"My holidays
on video!"

newspaper
journal
Nina is reading
the newspaper.

telephone
téléphone
Tess is speaking
on the telephone.

VCR
video cassette recorder
magnétoscope
There is a video
in the VCR.

Retrouve les mots anglais qui correspondent à ces silhouettes.

The bedroom

La chambre

alarm clock
réveil
"I hate alarm clocks!"

pillow
oreiller
Pillow fights are fun.

ring
sonner
The alarm clock
is ringing.

bed
lit
Betty is in bed.

quilt
couette
The cat is under
the quilt.

sheet
drap
Teddy is under
the sheet.

blanket
couverture
Teddy is under
the blanket.

switch off
éteindre
Mummy switches off
the light.

switch on
allumer
Simon switches on
the light.

Retrouve les mots anglais qui correspondent à ces silhouettes.

The bathroom

La salle de bains

bath

baignoire ; bain
Barbara is in the bath.

shower

douche
Shannon is having
a shower.

toothbrush
toothpaste

brosse à dents-dentifrice
Tom brushes his teeth
with a toothbrush
and toothpaste.

hairbrush

brosse à cheveux
Brenda brushes her
hair with a hairbrush.

soap

savon
Sophie uses soap.

towel

serviette
A big soft towel.

shampoo

shampooing
Willy washes his hair
with shampoo.

toilet

toilettes
Tom reads
in the toilet.

wash

laver ;
se laver
Tom
washes
with
soap.

The kitchen

La cuisine

bottle

bouteille

The bottle is empty.

cupboard

placard

Cups in the cupboard.

saucepan

casserole

Daddy is washing
a saucepan.

chair

chaise

Charles on a chair.

fridge

réfrigérateur

Milk goes
in the fridge.

table

table

A chicken on the table.

cup

tasse

Two cups.

oven

four

The chicken is in the
oven.

glass verre   **spoon** cuiller

knife couteau

plate assiette

fork fourchette

bowl bol

Retrouve les mots anglais qui correspondent à ces silhouettes.

The garden

Le jardin

garage

garage

The car is
in the garage.

lawn

pelouse

Leo cuts
the lawn.

swing

balançoire

Sidney is
on the swing.

gate

barrière ; portail

"Where is the gate?"

ladder

échelle

Larry is
on the
ladder.

pet

animal familier

"I love my pets!"

dog

chien

"I hate dogs!"

cat

chat

A cat on a roof.

tortoise

tortue

The tortoise is green.

Retrouve
les mots anglais
qui correspondent
à ces silhouettes.

Little things

Les petites choses

bag

sac

A small bag
in a big bag.

glue

colle

You can repair
things with glue.

match/matches

allumette/allumettes

Matches are
dangerous.

box

boîte

A dog in a box.

hammer

marteau

Henry has a hammer.

nail

clou

"Hit the nail,
not your finger!"

computer

ordinateur

Connor has
a computer.

jewel

bijou

Julia loves jewels.

photo,
photograph

photo, photographie

A birthday photo.

54

picture
image
Linda likes
picture books.

—

tool
outil
A hammer is a tool.

work
marcher, fonctionner
"It works!"

ring
bague
Four rings.

—

Biggles Riddle
5, Camberwell Street
London W10

envelope
enveloppe
An address
on an envelope.

—

postcard
carte postale
A postcard
for Peter.

—

rope
corde
Robert has a boat
on a rope.

letter
lettre
Letters
for Linda

stamp
timbre
A stamp
on an envelope.

Action !

Action !

break

casser

Brenda breaks everything!

carry

porter

Cary carries a big bag.

do

faire

Diana is doing exercises.

bring

amener, apporter

Granny brings sweets.

catch

attraper

Mr Jones always catches big fish!

drop

laisser tomber

Darren drops a glass.

build

construire

Bill builds houses.

cut

couper

Carl is cutting paper.

fill

remplir

Phil is filling the jug.

fold
plier

Fred is folding
a letter.

—

get
avoir, recevoir

Gwen gets a present.

—

give
donner

Greg gives Mummy
flowers.

give back
rendre

"Give back
the bicycle, please!"

hang up
suspendre

Hanna hangs up
her coat.

put
mettre

Paul puts a letter
in the box.

have
avoir

Harriet has a new car.

—

keep
garder

Kim wants to keep
the bicycle.

put down
poser

Paula puts down
her suitcases.

make

faire, fabriquer

Meg is making
a dress.

pour

verser

Penny is pouring
orange juice.

receive

recevoir

Grandma has received
a letter.

mix

mélanger

Mummy is mixing
eggs and milk.

pull

tirer

Polly is pulling
Paul's hair.

open

ouvrir

The teacher
is opening the door.

need

avoir besoin de

Nigel needs help.

push

pousser

Pat is pushing his car.

close

fermer

Clare is closing
the door.

repair
réparer
Roger repairs shoes.

take
prendre
Hanna is taking
her coat.

use
utiliser, se servir de
Harry is using
a hammer.

send
envoyer
Sam is sending
a letter.

throw
lancer
Ben is throwing
the ball.

look for
chercher
Kevin is looking for
his schoolbag.

find
trouver
Kevin finds
his schoolbag.

shake
secouer
Mr Bear is shaking
the tree.

try
essayer
"Can I try?"

Retrouve
les mots anglais
qui correspondent
à ces silhouettes.

Getting on with people

S'entendre avec les autres

bother

ennuyer, embêter

"Stop bothering me!"

help

aider

Harry is helping
his father.

look after

s'occuper de

Linda is looking
after her sister.

disturb

déranger

The children are
disturbing the baby.

kiss

embrasser

Mummy
is kissing Katie.

meet

rencontrer

Mark is pleased
to meet Martin.

agree

être d'accord

Alex agrees to play
with Agnes and Alan.

disagree

ne pas être d'accord

Dina and Dean
disagree.

argue

se disputer

"Stop arguing!"

Expressions

Expressions

Be careful!

Fais attention !

Leave me alone!

Laisse-moi !
Laissez-moi tranquille !

there is
there are

il y a

There is one dog.
There are six cats.

Good luck!

Bonne chance !

Do you want one?

Of course!

of course

bien sûr

What's
the matter?

Que se passe-t-il ?

It
doesn't
matter!

Ça ne fait rien !
Ce n'est pas
grave !

I am fed up!

J'en ai assez !

I don't
care!

Ça m'est égal !

Retrouve
les mots anglais
qui correspondent
à ces silhouettes.

In my opinion

À mon avis

good
bon, bien

better
meilleur, mieux

the best
le meilleur, le mieux

interesting
intéressant

exciting
passionnant

great
génial, super

fantastic
fantastique

boring
ennuyeux

funny
drôle

bad
mauvais

worse
plus mauvais, pire

the worst
le plus mauvais, le pire

easy
facile
It's easy!

—

difficult
difficile
It's difficult!

fair
juste
This is fair.

—

unfair
injuste
This is unfair.

pleasant
agréable
A pleasant dream.

—

unpleasant
désagréable
An unpleasant dream.

disgusting
dégoûtant
Dennis is disgusting!

horrible
horrible
This dog is horrible!

scary
effrayant
"Oh! This is scary!"

favourite
préféré
"My favourite doll!"

intelligent
intelligent
Ingrid is
an intelligent girl.

strange
étrange, bizarre
"Ah! This is strange!"

lovely
charmant,
agréable - joli
Lucy is
a lovely girl.

nice
gentil, sympathique,
joli - bon
The teacher
is nice.

pretty
joli
Peggy is
a pretty girl.

wonderful
merveilleux
A wonderful
night.

Retrouve
les mots anglais
qui correspondent
à ces silhouettes.

Opposites

Les contraires

alive
vivant
The cat is alive.

dead
mort
The cat is dead.

high
haut
It's high!

low
bas
It's low!

on
allumé
The radio is on.

off
éteint
The radio is off.

little
petit
A little mouse.

big
grand
A big elephant.

clean
propre
A clean dress.

dirty
sale
A dirty dress.

wet
mouillé
Wet feet.

dry
sec
Dry feet.

beautiful
beau,
magnifique
"It's beautiful!"

ugly
laid
"You are
ugly!"

empty
vide
The chocolate
box is empty.

full
plein
The bath is full.

new
neuf
"Look at my
new shoes!"

old
vieux
Olivia likes
old dresses.

heavy
lourd
This book
is heavy.

light
léger
Leaves
are light.

same
même, pareil
They have the
same trainers.

different
différent
Dennis and Dan
are different.

dark
sombre

light
clair

asleep
endormi
Arthur is asleep.

awake
éveillé
Alfred is awake.

deep
profond
The river is deep.

short
court
Charlotte
has short hair.

long
long
Lenny has a long scarf.

flat
plat
The road is flat.

enormous
énorme
"What an
enormous fish!"

tiny
minuscule, tout petit
A tiny insect.

thick
épais
The book is thick!

Retrouve les mots anglais qui correspondent à ces silhouettes.

At school

À l'école

alphabet

alphabet

Zorro knows
the alphabet.

class

classe

Cathy's class is going
on a picnic.

count

compter

Karl is counting.

blackboard

tableau

"Look at the
blackboard, please."

classroom

salle de classe

The children are
in the classroom.

desk

bureau

Daisy is at her desk.

chalk

craie

The chalk is white.

right

juste, bon, exact

This is right.

wrong

faux

This is wrong.

dictionary

dictionnaire
Dictionaries are big.

draw

dessiner
Dean is drawing.

drawing

dessin
"What a lovely
drawing!"

fight

se battre, se bagarrer
Fred and Felix
are fighting.

friend

ami, copain
Frances and Philip
are friends.

teacher

maître, maîtresse - professeur
The teacher is
in the classroom.

learn

apprendre
Laura is learning
a poem.

lesson

cours, leçon
A geometry lesson.

pupil

élève
Pupils go to school.

painter - paint
paintbrush
peintre - peindre - pinceau
A painter paints
with a paintbrush.

pencil
crayon à papier
Pam is writing
with a pencil.

playground
cour de récréation
The playground
is empty.

paper
papier
The paper is white.

play
jouer
"Who wants to play?"

playtime
récréation
It's playtime.

pen
stylo
Penny has a new pen.

work
travailler
William and Wendy
are working.

homework
devoirs
Holly is doing
her homework.

read
lire
The teacher
is reading a story.

show
montrer
The children
are showing a picture
to the teacher.

well
bien
Winnie sings well.

schoolbag
cartable
The schoolbags
are heavy.

teach
enseigner, apprendre
(à quelqu'un)
Tess is teaching
Charles to write.

Look,
I can write!

write
écrire
Willy can write.

book
livre
Brenda
loves books.

exercise book
cahier
Emily is writing in
her exercise book.

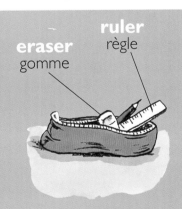

eraser
gomme

ruler
règle

pencil case
trousse

Retrouve
les mots anglais
qui correspondent
à ces silhouettes.

Sport

Les sports

champion

champion

"I am the champion!"

match

match

The match is over!

swimming pool

piscine

The swimming pool is deep.

competition

compétition

The winners of the competition.

race

course

Ready for the race!

team

équipe

Tom's football team.

win

gagner

"We are winning"

winner

gagnant, vainqueur

"We are the winners!"

lose

perdre

Sometimes you lose...

football
football

boxing
boxe

fencing
escrime

skiing
ski

tennis
tennis

rugby
rugby

pole vaulting
saut à la perche

gymnastics
gymnastique

judo
judo

basketball
basket

ice-skating
patinage

swimming
natation

Retrouve
les mots anglais
qui correspondent
à ces silhouettes.

Hobbies

Les loisirs

ball

ballon

Barbara plays
with a red ball.

card

carte

"Is this card OK?"

comics

bande dessinée

Calvin loves comics.

bicycle, bike

vélo

Bernard is always
riding his bicycle.

chess

jeu d'échecs

Chuck plays chess
with his dad.

dance

danser

Mr and Mrs Dunlop
like dancing.

camera

appareil-photo

"Look at the camera!"

circus

cirque

The circus is fun.

doll

poupée

Debbie has a big doll.

dress up
se déguiser
The children
are dressed up.

invite
inviter
Ian has invited
his friends.

picnic
pique-nique
A pizza for the picnic.

game
jeu
"I love this game!"

marble
bille
Marty and Minnie
are playing marbles.

puppet
marionnette
Peter is playing
with a puppet.

hide-and-seek
cache-cache
Hanna and Simon are
playing hide-and-seek.

museum
musée
Matthew visits
museums with his dad.

rollerblade
roller
Rollerblades
are dangerous!

show
spectacle
A magic show.

video game
jeu vidéo
Video games
are fun.

visit
visiter
Vicky visits Versailles.

theatre
théâtre
The theatre
is exciting.

cartoon
dessin animé
Cartoons are funny.

cinema
cinéma
There is a good film
at the cinema.

toy
jouet
Tina has a lot of toys.

actor-actress
acteur-actrice
Andy is an actor.

film
film
Dakota Jones
is a fantastic film.

Retrouve les mots anglais qui correspondent à ces silhouettes.

Music!

Musique!

band
groupe
Bob and Bart
play in a band.

guitar
guitare
Gus plays the guitar.

trumpet
trompette
Terry plays
the trumpet.

drum
tambour
Don plays drums.

piano
piano
Peter plays the piano.

violin
violon
Violet plays
the violin.

sing
chanter
John is singing...

song
chanson
his favourite song...

CD
CD
from his new CD.

77

Retrouve
les mots anglais
qui correspondent
à ces silhouettes.

Jobs

Les métiers

a farmer
un fermier

an architect
un architecte

a builder
un maçon

a plumber
un plombier

a baker
un boulanger

an engineer
un ingénieur

a reporter
une journaliste

a cameraman
un cameraman

a doctor
un docteur

a receptionist
un réceptioniste

a teacher
un professeur

a musician
un musicien

a policeman
un policier

**a computer
technician**
un informaticien

a banker
un banquier

a secretary
une secrétaire

78

become
devenir
Tracy wants
to become a teacher.

fireman/firemen
pompier/pompiers
A fireman fights fires.

nurse
infirmière
Nurses are nice.

butcher
boucher
A butcher sells meat.

grocer
épicier
A grocer sells food.

postman/postmen
facteur/facteurs
A postman
brings letters.

chemist
pharmacien
A chemist
sells medicine.

hairdresser
coiffeur
A hairdresser
cuts hair.

waiter
serveur
"Waiter, please!"

Retrouve
les mots anglais
qui correspondent
à ces silhouettes.

Shopping

Les courses

bargain
bonne affaire
"This is a bargain!"

cost
coûter
"It costs a lot!"

price
prix
The price is
on the box.

buy
acheter
Mr and Mrs Berry
buy a lot of food.

a note
un billet

a coin
une pièce

money
argent

purse
porte-monnaie
An empty purse...

change
monnaie
"Here's your change,
dear."

pay
payer
Polly pays
with a note.

sell
vendre
Steven sells flowers.

shop
magasin
Charles works
in a shoe shop.

shopkeeper
commercant
The baker
and the butcher
are shopkeepers.

spend
dépenser
Spencer spends
his money on sweets.

shop assistant
vendeur
The shop assistant
is young.

shopping
courses
Mummy is doing
the shopping.

supermarket
supermarché
Kiki is at
the supermarket.

free
gratuit
This water
is free.

cheap
bon marché
This water
is cheap.

expensive
cher
Rollerblades
are expensive!

Retrouve
les mots anglais
qui correspondent
à ces silhouettes.

In town

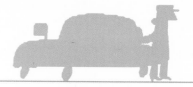

En ville

bank

banque

Billy is leaving
the bank...

church

église

There is a wedding
at the church.

market

marché

Mr Marlow shops
at the market.

building

immeuble, bâtiment

Big buildings.

hotel

hôtel

Harry is going
to the hotel.

office

bureau

Olivia works
in an office.

café

café

The Carters
are drinking coffee
in a café.

library

bibliothèque

Lily goes to the
library after school.

park

parc, square

Peggy and Paul are
playing in the park.

pavement
trottoir
There are two people
on the pavement.

post office
poste
Pam is going to
the post office.

street
rue
There is only one
car in the street.

police station
commissariat
A policeman in front
of the police station.

restaurant
restaurant
Mr Roberts is
at the restaurant.

town hall
mairie
The town hall
is pink.

city
grande ville

town
ville

capital
capitale

suburbs
banlieue

On the road

Sur la route

accident
accident
A car accident.

drive
conduire
Dean drives
an ambulance.

motorbike
moto
The motorbike is blue.

bus – bus stop
bus – arrêt de bus
The bus stops
at the bus stop.

engine
moteur
Emily is looking
at the engine.

motorway
autoroute
Cars go fast
on the motorway.

cross
traverser
Clare is crossing
the street.

helmet
casque
Helen has
a red helmet.

policeman
policier, agent de police
"Oh no,
a policeman!"

ride
faire du, monter à
(vélo, cheval)
Rick is riding
his bicycle.
Harold is riding
a horse.

road
route
Country roads
are pleasant.

taxi
taxi
The taxi is yellow.

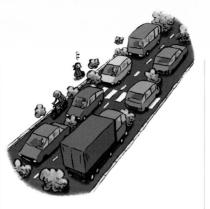

traffic
circulation
There is a lot
of traffic on the road.

traffic jam
embouteillage
Everybody hates
traffic jams.

tube, underground
métro
They are waiting
for the tube.

wheel
roue
A car has four wheels.

fast
rapide ; vite
The car is going fast.

slow
lent
The snail is slow.

Retrouve
les mots anglais
qui correspondent
à ces silhouettes.

Transport

Les transports

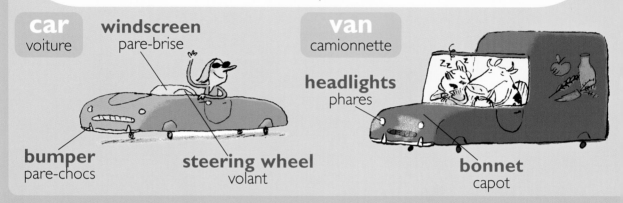

car
voiture

windscreen
pare-brise

van
camionnette

headlights
phares

bumper
pare-chocs

steering wheel
volant

bonnet
capot

bicycle, bike
vélo

handlebars
guidon

wheel
roue

pedal
pédale

motorbike
moto

saddle
selle

helm
casqu

train
train

passenger
passager

carriage
wagon

plane
avion

wing
aile

window
hublot

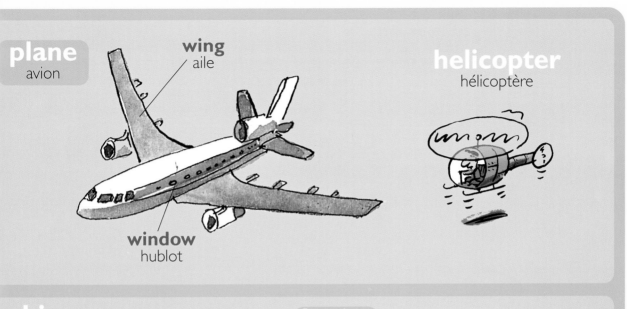

helicopter
hélicoptère

ship
bateau (grand)

funnel
cheminée

deck
pont

boats
bateaux

porthole
hublot

cabin
cabine

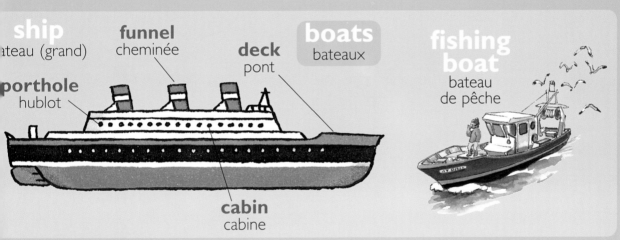

fishing boat
bateau de pêche

driver
conducteur

locomotive
locomotive

Retrouve les mots anglais qui correspondent à ces silhouettes.

Travelling

En voyage

airport

aéroport

Ann and Adam are
at the airport.

map

carte, plan

Mandy is looking
at the map.

suitcase

valise

Susan is carrying
a big suitcase.

holiday

vacances

"Hooray!
We are on holiday!"

miss

manquer, rater

Molly is going to
miss the train.

Tickets please!

ticket

billet, ticket

luggage

bagages

Luke has a lot
of luggage.

station

gare

There are many people
at the station.

travel

voyager

Tom travels by plane.

Retrouve les mots anglais qui correspondent à ces silhouettes.

Winter sports

Les sports d'hiver

ice
glace
An igloo on the ice.

ski
skier, faire du ski
Suzy and Simon
are skiing.

snow
neige
The children are
playing in the snow.

ice-skate
patin à glace - patiner
Ian loves ice-skating.

sledge - sled
faire de la luge
Sam is sledging.

snowman/
snowmen
bonhomme(s) de neige
"This snowman
is enormous!"

mountain
montagne
Martin at the top
of the mountain.

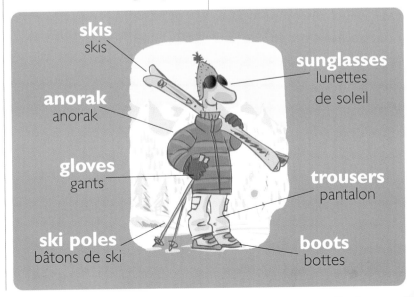

skis
skis

anorak
anorak

gloves
gants

ski poles
bâtons de ski

sunglasses
lunettes
de soleil

trousers
pantalon

boots
bottes

At the seaside

Au bord de la mer

beach

plage

Benny and Barbara
at the beach.

rock

rocher

A big rock.

sandcastle

château de sable

The children are
making a sandcastle.

crab

crabe

The crab is walking
on the sand.

sailing boat

voilier

The Smiths have a
sailing boat.

sea

mer

The sea is blue.

island

île

A small island.

sand

sable

Sam and Sally are
playing in the sand.

seaside

bord de mer

Summer
at the seaside.

shade
ombre
Daddy is in the shade.

shell
coquillage
A collection
of sea shells.

sunglasses
lunettes de soleil
Sam is wearing
sunglasses.

swim
nager
Simon is swimming.

swimsuit
maillot de bain
Suzy has
a red swimsuit.

wave
vague
A small boat
on a big wave.

diving mask
masque
de plongée

snorkel
tuba

net
épuisette

suitcase
valise

rubber ring
bouée

Retrouve
les mots anglais
qui correspondent
à ces silhouettes.

In the country

À la campagne

animal

animal

A cow is an animal.

flower

fleur

Flowers smell nice.

fox/foxes

renard/renards

Foxes like hens.

bird

oiseau

A big bird
and a small bird.

fly

voler

Birds fly.

frog

grenouille

Frogs jump.

butterfly/
butterflies

papillon/papillons

A yellow butterfly.

forest

forêt

The boys are playing
in the forest.

grass

herbe

Greg and Gwen are
playing in the grass.

insect

insecte

Insects are small.

owl

chouette - hibou

An owl on a branch.

tree

arbre

Trees have leaves.

leaf/leaves

feuille, feuilles

Leaves fall in autumn.

river

rivière

Rick in the river.

village

village

The village is near
the river.

mushroom

champignon

Some mushrooms
are dangerous!

squirrel

écureuil

A squirrel
on a branch.

wood

bois

A red bird in a wood.

Retrouve
les mots anglais
qui correspondent
à ces silhouettes.

On the farm

À la ferme

barn

grange

The children are
playing in the barn.

cock

coq

The cock says
cock-a-doodle-doo.

cow

vache

The cow is quiet.

donkey

âne

The horse is big,
the donkey is small.

duck

canard

The duck
is swimming.

farmer

fermier

The farmer
is in his farm.

field

champ

Two cows in a field.

goat

chèvre

Goats give milk.

hen

poule

Two hens and a cock.

horse
cheval
Horses eat grass.

pig
cochon
The pig is pink.

sheep/sheep
mouton/moutons
Sheep are white.

mouse/mice
souris/souris
Mice like cheese.

rabbit
lapin
Rabbits eat carrots.

tractor
tracteur
Tom has a tractor.

The farm
la ferme

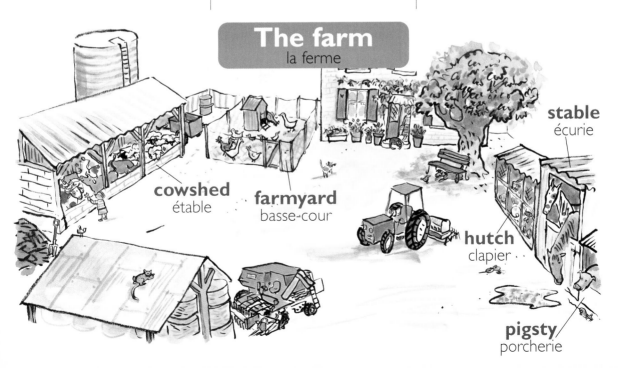

cowshed étable

farmyard basse-cour

stable écurie

hutch clapier

pigsty porcherie

Retrouve les mots anglais qui correspondent à ces silhouettes.

At the zoo

Au zoo

giraffe
girafe

camel
chameau

kangaroo
kangourou

crocodile
crocodile

elephant
éléphant

dolphin
dauphin

parrot
perroquet

eagle
aigle

monkey
singe

tiger
tigre

lion
lion

zebra
zèbre

penguin
pingouin

ostrich/ostriches
autruche

bear
ours

wolf/wolves
loup/loups

Retrouve
les mots anglais
qui correspondent
à ces silhouettes.

The weather

Le temps qu'il fait

blow

souffler

The wind is blowing.

cloud

nuage

The cloud is black.

rain

pleuvoir

"Yipee, it's raining!"

The weather

le temps

sunshine

grand soleil

snow

neige

thunderstorm

orage

wind

vent

rain

pluie

rainbow

arc-en-ciel

The rainbow
is beautiful.

shine

briller

The sun is shining.

storm

tempête

A storm on the sea.

umbrella

parapluie

A big brown umbrella.

The four seasons

spring
printemps

les quatre saisons

summer
été

autumn
automne

winter
hiver

cold
froid
"It's cold,
outside!"

warm
doux, chaud
"It's
warm,
inside!"

cool
frais
"It's cool!"

hot
(très, trop) chaud
"It's hot!"

Retrouve
les mots anglais
qui correspondent
à ces silhouettes.

The universe

L'univers

astronaut

astronaute

"Who are you?
I am an astronaut!"

Earth

Terre

The sun shines
on the Earth.

moon

lune

A man on the moon.

sky

ciel

The moon shines
in the sky at night.

spaceship

vaisseau spatial

An astronaut travels
in a spaceship.

star

étoile

Stars in the sky.

sun

soleil

The Earth moves
around the sun.

universe

univers

The universe
is very big.

world

monde

There is a map of the
world in the classroom.

Retrouve
les mots anglais
qui correspondent
à ces silhouettes.

Let's celebrate!

Faisons la fête!

birthday
anniversaire
"Happy birthday!"

fireworks
feu d'artifice
Fireworks
on the beach.

party
fête
Mr and Mrs Payne
are dancing at a party.

Christmas
Noël
Is it Christmas today?

Halloween
Halloween
Children dress up
for Halloween.

present
cadeau
A present for Penny.

Easter
Pâques
Two Easter eggs.

New Year
le Nouvel An
"Happy New Year!"

wedding
mariage
A wedding cake.

Time

Le temps qui passe

again

de nouveau, encore

"It's raining again!"

now

maintenant, tout de suite

Cinderella
must go now.

sometimes

quelquefois

Sometimes, Tom takes
his rabbit to school.

hurry

se dépêcher

"Hurry up Hannah!"

often

souvent

It is often cold
in winter.

soon

bientôt

Soon it will be
Christmas.

next

prochain

"Next year,
you will go there!"

ready

prêt

Rachel
is ready
for school.

stop

arrêter

"Stop crying,
my dear!"

Retrouve
les mots anglais
qui correspondent
à ces silhouettes.

then
ensuite
Minnie is eating
crisps. Then,
she will eat cake.

tonight
ce soir
Ted and Tess are
going out tonight.

wait (for)
attendre
William is waiting
for Fanny.

when
quand
When it rains,
Wendy wears
her yellow raincoat.

morning
matin
Morty wakes up early
in the morning.

afternoon
après-midi
In the afternoon,
Albert plays football.

day
jour
"Today is
a sunny day!"

night
nuit
"Tonight is
a quiet night!"

evening
soir
In the evening, Albert
watches television.

yesterday
hier
Yesterday, William
wrote a letter.

before
avant
Bob before
the match.

after
après
Bob after
the match.

today
aujourd'hui
Today, William
is sending his letter.

always
toujours
Alice always sleeps
with her bear.

never
jamais
Nelly never travels
without her bear.

tomorrow
demain
Tomorrow, Tom
will read the letter.

still
encore, toujours
Steven
is still asleep.

usually
d'habitude
Polly usually brushes
her teeth after meals.

early
tôt
The cock gets up
early!

late
tard, en retard
"It's late,
we are late!"

start
commencer
The pupils are starting
their drawings.

finish
terminer
The pupils
have finished
their drawings.

last year
l'année dernière
Last year,
Lucy was five.

next year
l'année prochaine
Next year,
Lucy will be seven.

slowly
lentement
The turtle
moves slowly.

———

quickly
vite, rapidement
The car goes quickly.

———

quick
vite
"Quick! Come quick!
I need help!"

Here and there

Ici et là

around

autour

The children
are running
around Richard.

next to

à côté de

Mary is sitting
next to her Mummy.

place

place

"This is my place!"

at

à, chez

Dennis at the doctor's.

over

par-dessus

The plane is flying
over the city.

through

à travers

The road goes
through the village.

between

entre

Benny is between
his mum and his dad.

where

où

"Where is
she?"

here

ici

"She is not
here!"

there

là

"She is not
there!"

in front of
devant
The Queen is always
in front of her mirror.

behind
derrière
Rita
is behind Ron.

on
sur
The car is on the bridge

everywhere - nowhere
partout - nulle part
Emily is looking everywhere. Ned is nowhere.

under
sous
The cat is
under the table.

near
près
Nancy lives
near the park.

far
loin
But she lives
far from the school.

inside-outside
à l'intérieur - à l'extérieur
Woofy is inside.
Spike is outside

in
dans
"Come in, Rex!"

top
sommet
Tom at the top!

bottom
fond
Fish at the bottom
of the sea.

out
dehors, hors de
"You stay out!"

way
direction
Which way
is it?

left
à gauche
"Not on
the left…"

up - down
en haut - en bas
Gus is going up.
Glenda is going down.

right
à droite
"Not on
the right…"

straight on
tout droit
"Let's go
straight on!"

From the beginning to the end

Du début jusqu'à la fin

Retrouve les mots anglais qui correspondent à ces silhouettes.

begin
commencer
It's beginning to rain.

middle
milieu
In the middle
of the night.

beginning
début
It's the beginning
of the match.

follow
suivre
"Follow me,
children!"

turn
tour
"It's my turn!"

end
fin
It's the end
of the match.

first
premier
A
is the first letter
of the alphabet.

second
second
Fred is first.
Simon
is second.

third
troisième
Theo is third.

last
dernier
Leo is always
the last.

Retrouve
les mots anglais
qui correspondent
à ces silhouettes.

Quantities

Les quantités

all

tout, tous, toutes

All the children
want sweets.

every

chaque

They want sweets
every day!

less

moins

"Less, please!"

enough

assez

There is
enough milk!

half

moitié

"Half for you,
half for me!"

more

plus

"More, please!"

a lot

beaucoup (de)

"A lot of spaghetti,
please!"

a little

un peu (de)

"A little spaghetti,
please!"

no

pas de

"No spaghetti,
thank you!"

nearly

presque

Nick has nearly finished.

—

some

certains - quelques

Some children are big some are small.

too

trop

It's too difficult!

piece

morceau, bout

"Who wants a piece of pie?"

—

how many?

combien (nombre)

"How many apples?"

—

how much?

combien (quantité)

"How much ice-cream?"

—

rest

reste

"Can I have the rest?"

too many

trop de (nombre)

"Too many apples!"

too much

trop de (quantité)

"Too much ice-cream!"

A little grammar

Un peu de grammaire

LES PRONOMS

En anglais, il n'y a pas de différences entre le **tu** et le **vous** : **you**
Il existe un pronom pour le **neutre** : **it**

I → je	**me** → me, moi	**my** → mon, ma, mes
you → tu	**you** → te, toi	**your** → ton, ta, tes
he → il	**him** → le, lui	**his** → son, sa, ses
she → elle	**her** → la, lui	**her** → son, sa, ses
it → il, elle	**it** → le, la, lui	**its** → son, sa, ses
us → nous	**us** → nous	**our** → notre, nos
you → vous	**you** → vous	**your** → votre, vos
they → ils, elles	**them** → les, eux, leur	**their** → leur, leurs

LES ARTICLES

a → un, une s'utilise devant les mots commençant par une **consonne**	**an** → un, une s'utilise devant les mots commençant par une **voyelle**	Au **pluriel** il n'y a pas d'articles

a pear → une poire

an apple → une pomme

apples → des pommes

a pig → un cochon

an elephant → un éléphant
an exercise book
→ un cahier

elephants → des éléphants
pigs → des cochons

a cat → un chat

a car → une voiture

En anglais on utilise le même article **the** pour le **masculin**, le **féminin** et le **pluriel**

the ⇢ le, la, les

the boy ⇢ le garçon | **the** girl ⇢ la fille | **the** children ⇢ les enfants

Pour désigner quelque chose on utilise
this et **that** (au **singulier**) et **these** et **those** (au **pluriel**)

this cat ⇢ **ce** chat
(le chat est proche)

that dog ⇢ **ce** chien
(le chien est plus loin)

these cats ⇢ **ces** chats
(les chats sont proches)
those dogs ⇢ **ces** chiens
(les chiens sont loin)

LES QUANTITÉS

Pour poser des questions sur une **quantité**, on utilise
how many et **how much** ⇢ combien de

Pour indiquer une **quantité** on utilise les mots
a few, **some**, **much**, **a lot of**, **many**, **no**

Quand on peut compter les **objets**,
on utilise **how many** :

Quand on ne peut pas compter les **quantités**,
on utilise **much** :

how many books ?
⇢ **combien de** livres

how much milk ?
⇢ **combien de** lait

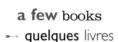

a few books
⇢ **quelques** livres

some books
⇢ **des** livres

a little milk
⇢ **un peu de** lait

some milk
⇢ **du** lait

many books
⇢ **beaucoup de** livres

a lot of books
⇢ **beaucoup de** livres

much milk
⇢ **beaucoup de** lait

a lot of milk
⇢ **beaucoup de** lait

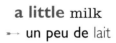

too much milk
⇢ **trop de** lait

no milk ⇢ **pas de** lait

too many books
⇢ **trop de** livres

LES COMPARAISONS

Il y a deux manières d'exprimer **plus** et **moins**.

Si l'adjectif ou l'adverbe est **long** on utilise **more** et **less** :

| interesting | **more** interesting | **less** interesting |
| intéressant | **plus** intéressant | **moins** intéressant |

Si l'adjectif ou l'adverbe est **court** on ajoute **er** à la fin du mot.

small
petit

happy
heureux

small**er**
plus petit

happi**er**
plus heureux

LES VERBES

To **be** → Être

I **am** → je suis
you **are** → tu es
he **is** → il est
she **is** → elle est
it **is** → il est, elle est, c'est
we **are** → nous sommes
you **are** → vous êtes
they **are** → il sont, elles sont

I **am not** → je ne suis pas
you **are not** → you **aren't** → tu n'es pas
he **is not** → he **isn't** → il n'est pas
she **is not** → she **isn't** → elle n'est pas
it **is not** → it **isn't** → il, elle, ce n'est pas
we **are not** → we **aren't** → nous ne sommes pas
you **are not** → you **aren't** → vous n'êtes pas
they **are not** → they **aren't** → ils, elles ne sont pas

To **have** → Avoir

I **have** → j'ai
you **have** → tu as
he **has** → il a
she **has** → elle a
it **has** → il, elle a
we **have** → nous avons
you **have** → vous avez
they **have** → ils, elles ont

I **have not** → I **haven't** → je n'ai pas
you **have not** → you **haven't** → tu n'as pas
he **has not** → he **hasn't** → il n'a pas
she **has not** → she **hasn't** → elle n'a pas
it **has not** → it **hasn't** → il, elle n'a pas
we **have not** → we **haven't** → nous n'avons pas
you **have not** → you **haven't** → vous n'avez pas
they **have not** → they **haven't** → ils, elles n'ont pas

To **do** → Faire

I **do** → je fais
you **do** → tu fais
he **does** → il fait
she **does** → elle fait
it **does** → il, elle fait
we **do** → nous faisons
you **do** → vous faites
they **do** → ils, elles font

I **do not** → I **don't** → je ne fais pas
you **do not** → you **don't** → tu ne fais pas
he **does not** → he **doesn't** → il ne fait pas
she **does not** → she **doesn't** → elle ne fait pas
it **does not** → it **doesn't** → il, elle ne fait pas
we **do not** → we **don't** → nous ne faisons pas
you **do not** → you **don't** → vous ne faites pas
they **do not** → they **don't** → ils, elles ne font pas

Le présent composé

Il y a deux présents en anglais. Quand **on parle de ce qu'on est en train de faire**
on utilise **to be** avant le verbe et **ing** à la fin :

I **am** play**ing** ⇥ je joue, je suis en train de jouer
you **are** play**ing** ⇥ tu joues, tu es en train de jouer
he **is** play**ing** ⇥ il joue, il est en train de jouer
she **is** play**ing** ⇥ elle joue, elle est en train de jouer
it **is** play**ing** ⇥ il, elle joue, il, elle est en train de jouer
we **are** play**ing** ⇥ nous jouons, nous sommes en train de jouer
you **are** play**ing** ⇥ vous jouez, vous êtes en train de jouer
they **are** play**ing** ⇥ ils, elles jouent, ils, elles sont en train de jouer

I **am not** play**ing** ⇥ je ne joue pas, je ne suis pas en train de jouer...

La forme négative

Pour mettre un verbe à la **forme négative**,
on utilise **do not** :

I **play** ⇥ je joue

I **do not play**
→ I **don't play**
⇥ je ne joue pas

L'impératif

Go ⇥ Vas-y

Do not go
→ **don't go**
⇥ N'y va pas

Let's go
⇥ Allons-y

you **can** do it → tu **peux** le faire

you **cannot** do it → you **can't** do it
→ tu **ne peux pas** le faire

Must → devoir

you **must** do it → tu **dois** le faire

you **must not** do it
→ you **musn't** do it
→ tu **ne dois pas** le faire

Pour bien prononcer les mots anglais

Les principaux sons

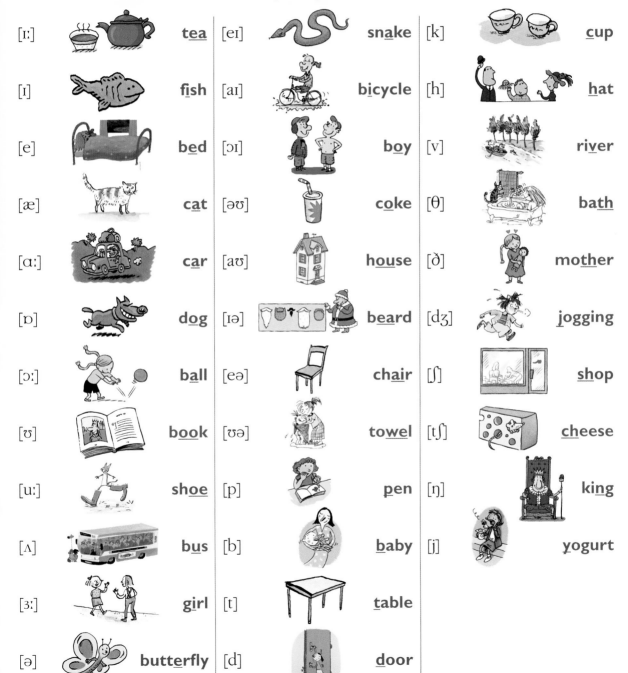

[ɪː] tea	[eɪ] snake	[k] cup
[ɪ] fish	[aɪ] bicycle	[h] hat
[e] bed	[ɔɪ] boy	[v] river
[æ] cat	[əʊ] coke	[θ] bath
[ɑː] car	[aʊ] house	[ð] mother
[ɒ] dog	[ɪə] beard	[dʒ] jogging
[ɔː] ball	[eə] chair	[ʃ] shop
[ʊ] book	[ʊə] towel	[tʃ] cheese
[uː] shoe	[p] pen	[ŋ] king
[ʌ] bus	[b] baby	[j] yogurt
[ɜː] girl	[t] table	
[ə] butterfly	[d] door	

INDEX
ANGLAIS - FRANÇAIS

A

a [ə] un, une 112

accident [ˈæksɪdənt] accident 84

action [ˈækʃən] action 56

actor [ˈæktə] acteur 76

actress [ˈæktrɪs] actrice 76

address [əˈdres] adresse 47

adult [ˈædʌlt] adulte 14

afraid (be ~) [əˈfreɪd]
avoir peur 26

after [ˈɑːftə] après 104

afternoon [ˈɑːftəˈnuːn]
après-midi 7, 103

again [əˈgen] à nouveau 102

agree [əˈgriː] être d'accord 60

airport [ˈɛəpɔːt] aéroport 88

alarm clock [əˈlɑːm klɒk]
réveil 12, 50

alive [əˈlaɪv] vivant 65

all [ɔːl] tout, tous, toutes 110

alphabet [ˈælfəbet] alphabet 68

always [ˈɔːlweɪz] toujours 104

an [ən] un, une 112

and [ænd] et 8

angry [ˈæŋgrɪ] en colère 26

animal [ˈænɪməl] animal 92

ankle [ˈæŋkl] cheville 18

answer [ˈɑːnsə] réponse ;
répondre 32

anorak [ˈænəræk] anorak 89

apple [ˈæpl] pomme 45

April [ˈeɪprəl] avril 13

architect [ˈɑːkɪtekt]
architecte 78

argue [ˈɑːgjuː] se disputer 60

arm [ɑːm] bras 18

armchair [ˈɑːmtʃɛə] fauteuil 48

around [əˈraʊnd] autour de 106

ashamed (be ~) [əˈʃeɪmd]
avoir honte 26

ask [ɑːsk] demander 32

asleep [əˈsliːp] endormi 35, 67

astronaut [ˈæstrənɔːt]
astronaute 100

at [æt] à, chez 106

atishoo [əˈtɪʃuː] atchoum 20

attic [ˈætɪk] grenier 46

August [ˈɔːgəst] août 13

aunt [ɑːnt] tante 16

autumn [ˈɔːtəm] automne 99

awake [əˈweɪk] (r)éveillé 67

B

baby [ˈbeɪbɪ] bébé 14

back [bæk] dos 18

bacon [ˈbeɪkən] bacon 41

bad [bæd] mauvais 63

bag [bæg] sac 54

baker [ˈbeɪkə] boulanger 78

ball [bɔːl] ballon 74

banana [bəˈnɑːnə] banane 45

band [bænd] orchestre 77

bank [bæŋk] banque 82

banker [ˈbæŋkə] banquier 78

bargain [ˈbɑːgɪn] affaire 80

barn [bɑːn] grange 94

basketball [ˈbɑːskɪt bɔːl]
basket 73

bath [bɑːθ] baignoire ; bain 35, 51

bathroom [ˈbɑːθrʊm] salle de
bains 51

be [biː] être 116

beach [biːtʃ] plage 90

bean [biːn] haricot 44

bear [bɛə] ours 97

beautiful [ˈbjuːtɪfʊl] beau 66

because [bɪˈkɒz] parce que 8

become [bɪˈkʌm], **became,
become** devenir 79

bed [bed] lit 50

bedroom [ˈbedrʊm] chambre
50

beef [biːf] bœuf 40

before [bɪˈfɔː] avant 104

begin [bɪˈgɪn], **began, begun**
commencer 109

beginning [bɪˈgɪnɪŋ] début 109

begun [bɪˈgʌn] → begin

behind [bɪˈhaɪnd] derrière 107

believe [bɪˈliːv] croire 31

belt [belt] ceinture 36

best [best] le meilleur,
la meilleure, le mieux 62

better [ˈbetə] meilleur, mieux
62

between [bɪˈtwiːn] entre 106

bicycle [ˈbaɪsɪkl] vélo 74, 86

big [bɪg] grand 65

bike [baɪk] vélo 74, 86

bird [bɜːd] oiseau 92

birthday [ˈbɜːθdeɪ]
anniversaire 101

biscuit [ˈbɪskɪt] biscuit 42

black [blæk] noir 11

blackboard [ˈblækbɔːd]
tableau noir 68

blanket [ˈblæŋkɪt] couverture 50

blood [blʌd] sang 19

blouse [blaʊz] chemisier 36

blow [bləʊ], **blew, blown** souffler 98

blue [bluː] bleu 11

boat [bəʊt] petit bateau 87

body [ˈbɒdɪ] corps 18

bonnet [ˈbɒnɪt] capot 86

book [bʊk] livre 71

bookshelf/bookshelves [ˈbʊkʃelf] rayonnages 48

boot [buːt] botte 36, 89

bored (be ~) [bɔːd] s'ennuyer 26

boring [ˈbɔːrɪŋ] ennuyeux 62

bother [ˈbɒðə] ennuyer, embêter 60

bottle [ˈbɒtl] bouteille 52

bottom [ˈbɒtəm] derrière, fesses 18 ; fond 108

box/boxes [bɒks] boîte 54

boxing [ˈbɒksɪŋ] boxe 73

boy [bɔɪ] garçon 14

brave [breɪv] courageux 26

bread [bred] pain 39

break [breɪk], **broke, broken** casser 56

breakfast [ˈbrekfəst] petit déjeuner 38, 39

bring [brɪŋ], **brought, brought** amener, apporter 56

brother [ˈbrʌðə] frère 16

brown [braʊn] marron 11

brush [brʌʃ] brosse, brosser 51

build [bɪld], **built, built** construire 56

builder [ˈbɪldə] maçon 78

building [ˈbɪldɪŋ] bâtiment, immeuble 82

bumper [ˈbʌmpə] pare-chocs 86

bus [bʌs] autobus, bus 84

busy [ˈbɪzɪ] occupé 34

but [bʌt] mais 8

butcher [ˈbʊtʃə] boucher 79

butter [ˈbʌtə] beurre 39

butterfly [ˈbʌtəflaɪ] papillon 92

buy [baɪ], **bought, bought** acheter 80

bye [ˈbaɪ] au revoir 7

bye-bye [ˈbaɪ baɪ] au revoir 7

C

cabbage [ˈkæbɪdʒ] chou 44

cabin [ˈkæbɪn] cabine 87

café [ˈkæfeɪ] café (lieu) 82

cake [keɪk] gâteau 42

call [kɔːl] appeler 32

camel [ˈkæməl] chameau 96

camera [ˈkæmərə] appareil photo 74

cameraman [ˈkæmərəmən] cameraman 78

can [kæn] pouvoir 118

cap [kæp] casquette 36

capital [ˈkæpɪtl] capitale 83

car [kɑː] voiture 86

card [kɑːd] carte 74

cardigan [ˈkɑːdɪgən] gilet 36

careful (be ~) [ˈkɛəfʊl] faire attention 61

carpet [ˈkɑːpɪt] tapis 48

carrot [ˈkærət] carotte 44

carriage [ˈkærɪdʒ] wagon 86

carry [ˈkærɪ] porter 56

cartoon [kɑːˈtuːn] dessin animé 76

cat [kæt] chat 53

catch [kætʃ], **caught, caught** attraper 56

cauliflower [ˈkɒlɪflaʊə] chou-fleur 44

CD [ˈsiːdiː] CD 77

celebrate [ˈselɪbreɪt] fêter, faire la fête 101

cellar [ˈselə] cave 46

cereal [ˈsɪərɪəl] céréale 39

chair [tʃɛə] chaise 52

chalk [tʃɔːk] craie 68

champion [ˈtʃæmpjən] champion 72

change [tʃeɪndʒ] monnaie 80

cheap [tʃiːp] pas cher 81

check [tʃek] vérifier 23

cheek [tʃiːk] joue 18

cheese [tʃiːz] fromage 40

chemist [ˈkemɪst] pharmacien 79

cherry [ˈtʃerɪ] cerise 45

chess [tʃes] jeu d'échecs 74

chest [tʃest] poitrine 18

chicken [ˈtʃɪkɪn] poulet 40

child/children [tʃaɪld] [ˈtʃɪldrən] enfant(s) 14, 17

chimney [ˈtʃɪmnɪ] cheminée extérieure 46

chin [tʃɪn] menton 18

chips [tʃɪps] frites 40

chocolate [ˈtʃɒklɪt] chocolat 42

Christmas [ˈkrɪsməs] Noël 101

church [tʃɜːtʃ] église 82

cider [ˈsaɪdə] cidre 43

cinema [ˈsɪnəmə] cinéma 76

circle [ˈsɜːkl] cercle 11

circus [ˈsɜːkəs] cirque 74

city [ˈsɪtɪ] (grande) ville 83

class [klɑːs] classe 68

classroom ['klɑːsrʊm]
salle de classe 68

clean [kliːn] propre 65

clever ['klevə] malin, maligne 26

climb [klaɪm] grimper 24

close [kləʊz] fermer 58

clothes [kləʊðz] vêtements 36

cloud [klaʊd] nuage 98

coat [kəʊt] manteau 36

cocoa ['kəʊkəʊ]
chocolat chaud 43

cock [kɒk] coq 94

coffee ['kɒfɪ] café 39, 43

coin [kɔɪn] pièce de monnaie 80

cold [kəʊld] rhume 22 ; froid 99
be ~ avoir froid 21

colour ['kʌlə] couleur 11

come [kʌm], came, come
venir 25

come back [kʌm bæk]
revenir 25

come down [kʌm daʊn]
descendre 25

come in [kʌm ɪn] entrer 25

comfortable ['kʌmfətəbl]
confortable 48

comics ['kɒmɪks]
bande dessinée, BD 74

competition [ˌkɒmpɪ'tɪʃən]
compétition 72

computer [kəm'pjuːtə]
ordinateur 54

computer technician
[kəm'pjuːtə tek'nɪʃən]
informaticien 78

cook [kʊk] cuisiner, cuire 38

cool [kuːl] frais, fraîche 98

cost [kɒst], cost, cost coûter 80

cough [kɒf] tousser 23

count [kaʊnt] compter 68

country ['kʌntrɪ] campagne 92

of course [kɔːs] bien sûr 31, 61

cousin ['kʌzn] cousin, cousine 16

cow [kaʊ] vache 94

cowshed [kaʊʃed] étable 95

crab [kræb] crabe 90

crocodile ['krɔkədaɪl]
crocodile 96

cross [krɒs] traverser 84

cry [kraɪ] pleurer 27

cucumber ['kjuːkʌmbə]
concombre 44

cup [kʌp] tasse 52

cupboard ['kʌbəd] armoire,
placard 52

curly ['kɜːlɪ] bouclé 19

curtain ['kɜːtn] rideau 48

cushion ['kʊʃən] coussin 48

custard ['kʌstəd]
crème anglaise 42

cut [kʌt], cut, cut couper 56

D

dad [dæd] papa 17

daddy ['dædɪ] papa 17

dance [dɑːns] danser 74

dark [dɑːk] sombre 66

darling ['dɑːlɪŋ] chéri(e) 6

daughter ['dɔːtə] fille 17

day [deɪ] jour 12, 34, 103

dead [ded] mort, morte 65

dear [dɪə] cher, chère 6

December [dɪ'sembə]
décembre 13

deep [diːp] profond 67

delicious [dɪ'lɪʃəs] délicieux 38

dentist ['dentɪst] dentiste 22

desk [desk] bureau 68

diamond ['daɪəmənd]
losange 11

dictionary ['dɪkʃənrɪ]
dictionnaire 69

different ['dɪfrənt] différent 66

difficult ['dɪfɪkəlt] difficile 63

dinner ['dɪnə] dîner 35, 38

dirty ['dɜːtɪ] sale 65

disagree [ˌdɪsə'griː]
ne pas être d'accord 60

disappointed [ˌdɪsə'pɔɪntɪd]
déçu 27

disgusting [dɪs'gʌstɪŋ]
dégoûtant 64

disturb [dɪs'tɜːb] déranger 60

diving mask ['daɪvɪŋ mɑːsk]
masque de plongée 91

divorced [dɪ'vɔːst] divorcé 17

do [duː] faire 56, 116

doctor ['dɒktə] docteur 22, 78

dog [dɒg] chien 53

doll [dɒl] poupée 74

dolphin ['dɒlfɪn] dauphin 96

donkey ['dɒŋkɪ] âne 94

door [dɔː] porte 46

down [daʊn] en bas 108

downstairs [daʊnstɛəs]
en bas (des escaliers),
au rez-de-chaussée 47

draw [drɔː], drew, drawn
dessiner 69

drawer ['drɔːə] tiroir 48

drawing ['drɔːɪŋ] dessin 69

dress [dres] robe 37

dressed [drest] habillé 37
  get ~ s'habiller 35, 37
dress up ['dres ʌp]
se déguiser 75
drink [drɪŋk], **drank, drunk**
boire 38
drink [drɪŋk] boisson 43
drive [draɪv], **drove, driven**
conduire 84
driver ['draɪvə] conducteur 87
drop [drɒp] laisser tomber 56
drum [drʌm] tambour 77
dry [draɪ] sec, sèche 65
duck [dʌk] canard 94
dungarees [ˌdʌŋɡə'riːz]
salopette 36

E
eagle ['iːɡl] aigle 96
ear [ɪə] oreille 18
early ['ɜːlɪ] tôt 105
Earth [ɜːθ] Terre 100
Easter ['iːstə] Pâques 101
easy ['iːzɪ] facile 63
eat [iːt], **ate, eaten** manger 34, 38
egg [eɡ] œuf 41
eight [eɪt] huit 10
eighteen [eɪ'tiːn] dix-huit 10
eighty ['eɪtɪ] quatre-vingts 10
elbow ['elbəʊ] coude 18
elephant ['elɪfənt] éléphant 96
eleven [ɪ'levn] onze 10
empty ['emptɪ] vide 66
end [end] fin 109
engine ['endʒɪn] moteur 84
engineer [ˌendʒɪ'nɪə]
ingénieur 78

enormous [ɪ'nɔːməs]
énorme 67
enough [ɪ'nʌf] assez (de) 110
envelope ['envələʊp]
enveloppe 55
eraser [ɪ'reɪzə] gomme 71
even ['iːvən] même 8
evening ['iːvnɪŋ] soir 103
every ['evrɪ] chaque, tous,
toutes 110
everywhere ['evrɪwɛə]
partout 107
examine [ɪɡ'zæmɪn]
examiner 23
excited [ɪk'saɪtɪd] excité,
agité 27
exciting [ɪk'saɪtɪŋ]
passionnant 62
excuse me [ɪks'kjuːz miː]
pardon 6
exercise book ['eksəsaɪz bʊk]
cahier 71
expensive [ɪks'pensɪv] cher 81
expression [ɪks'preʃən]
expression 61
eye [aɪ] œil 18

F
face [feɪs] visage 19
fair [fɛə] juste 63
fall [fɔːl], **fell, fallen** tomber 24
family ['fæmɪlɪ] famille 16
fantastic [fæn'tæstɪk]
fantastique 62
far [fɑː] loin 107
farm [fɑːm] ferme 94, 95
farmer ['fɑːmə] fermier 78, 94

farmyard ['fɑːmjɑːd]
basse-cour 95
fast [fɑːst] rapide, vite 85
fat [fæt] gros, grosse 14
father ['fɑːðə] père 16
favourite ['feɪvərɪt] préféré 64
February ['februərɪ] février 13
feel [fiːl], **felt, felt** sentir ;
se sentir 23, 27
feeling ['fiːlɪŋ] sentiment 26
fencing ['fensɪŋ] escrime 73
field [fiːld] champ 94
fifteen [fɪf'tiːn] quinze 10
fifty ['fɪftɪ] cinquante 10
fight [faɪt], **fought, fought**
se battre, se bagarrer 69
fill [fɪl] remplir 56
film [fɪlm] film 76
find [faɪnd], **found, found**
trouver 59
finger ['fɪŋɡə] doigt 18
finish ['fɪnɪʃ] finir, terminer 105
fire ['faɪə] feu 48
fireman ['faɪəmən] / **firemen**
pompier(s) 79
fireplace ['faɪəpleɪs]
cheminée 48
fireworks ['faɪəwɜːks]
feu d'artifice 101
first [fɜːst] premier 109
fish [fɪʃ] poisson 40
fishing ['fɪʃɪŋ] pêche 87
five [faɪv] cinq 10
flat [flæt] appartement 47 ;
plat 67
floor [flɔː] plancher, sol 48
flour ['flaʊə] farine 40
flower ['flaʊə] fleur 92

fly [flaɪ], **flew, flown** voler 92

fold [fəʊld] plier 57

follow ['fɒləʊ] suivre 109

food [fuːd] nourriture 40

foot/feet [fʊt] pied(s) 18

football ['fʊtbɔːl] football 73

for [fɔː] pour 8

forehead ['fɒrɪd] front 18

forest ['fɒrɪst] forêt 92

forget [fə'get], **forgot, forgotten** oublier 30

fork [fɔːk] fourchette 52

forty ['fɔːtɪ] quarante 10

four [fɔː] quatre 10

fourteen [fɔː'tiːn] quatorze 10

fox/foxes [fɒks] renard(s) 92

free [friː] gratuit 81

Friday ['fraɪdɪ] vendredi 13

fridge [frɪdʒ] réfrigérateur 52

friend [frend] ami, copain 69

frightened ['fraɪtnd] effrayé 27

frog [frɒg] grenouille 92

from [frɒm] de 9

front [frʌnt] :in ~ of devant 107

fruit [fruːt] fruit 45

fruit juice [fruːt dʒuːs] jus de fruit 43

full [fʊl] plein 66

fun [fʌn] :have ~ s'amuser 35

funnel [fʌnl] cheminée (de bateau) 87

funny ['fʌnɪ] drôle, amusant 62

furniture ['fɜːnɪtʃə] meubles 46

G

game [geɪm] jeu 75

garage ['gærɑːʒ] garage 53

garden ['gɑːdn] jardin 53

gate [geɪt] barrière, portail 53

get [get], **got, gotten** avoir, recevoir, obtenir 57

get dressed [get drest] s'habiller 35, 37

get married [get 'mærɪd] se marier 17

get on [get ɒn] s'entendre (avec quelqu'un) 60

get up [get ʌp] se lever 34

giraffe [dʒɪ'rɑːf] girafe 96

girl [gɜːl] fille 14

give [gɪv], **gave, given** donner 57

give back [gɪv bæk] rendre 57

glad [glæd] ravi 28

glass [glɑːs] verre 52

glove [glʌv] gant 89

glue [gluː] colle 54

go [gəʊ], **went, gone** aller 24, 34

goat [gəʊt] chèvre 94

good [gʊd] bon, bonne, bien 62

good afternoon [gʊd 'ɑːftə'nuːn] bon après-midi 7

goodbye [gʊd'baɪ] au revoir 7

good evening [gʊd 'iːvnɪŋ] bonsoir 7

good luck ! [gʊd lʌk] bonne chance ! 61

good morning [gʊd 'mɔːnɪŋ] bonjour 7

goodnight [gʊd'naɪt] bonne nuit 7

grandfather ['grænfɑːðə] grand-père 16

grandmother ['grænmʌðə] grand-mère 16

grandparents ['grænpɛərənts] grands-parents 16

grapes [greɪps] raisin 45

grass [grɑːs] herbe 92

great [greɪt] génial, super 62

green [griːn] vert 11

grey [greɪ] gris 11

grocer ['grəʊsə] épicier 79

guess [ges] deviner 30

guitar [gɪ'tɑː] guitare 77

gymnastics [dʒɪm'næstɪks] gymnastique 73

H

ha ha [hɑː hɑː] hi hi 20

hair [hɛə] cheveux 18, 19

hairbrush ['hɛəbrʌʃ] brosse à cheveux 51

hairdresser ['hɛədresə] coiffeur 79

half/halves [hɑːf] moitié(s) 110

ham [hæm] jambon 40

hamburger ['hæmˌbɜːgə] hamburger 41

hammer ['hæmə] marteau 54

hand [hænd] main 18

handlebars ['hændlbɑːz] guidon 86

hang up [hæŋ ʌp], **hung, hung** suspendre, accrocher 57

happy ['hæpɪ] heureux 28

hard [hɑːd] dur 20

hat [hæt] chapeau 37

hate [heɪt] détester 26

have [hæv]**, had, had** avoir 57
he [hi:] il 112
head [hed] tête 18
headlight ['hedlaɪt] phare 86
health [helθ] santé 22
healthy ['helθɪ] en bonne
santé 22
hear [hɪə] entendre 20
heavy ['hevɪ] lourd 66
heel [hi:l] talon 18
helicopter ['helɪkɒptə]
hélicoptère 87
hello [hə'ləʊ] bonjour, salut 7
helmet ['helmɪt] casque 84
help [help] aider 60
hen [hen] poule 94
her [hɜ:] la, lui (personne) ;
son, sa, ses (à elle) 112
here [hɪə] ici 106
hide-and-seek [haɪd ænd
si:k] cache-cache 75
high [haɪ] haut 65
him [hɪm] le, lui 112
hip [hɪp] hanche 18
his [hɪz] son, sa, ses (à lui) 112
hobby ['hɒbɪ] hobby, loisir 74
holiday ['hɒlədɪ] vacances 88
home [həʊm] maison 46
homework ['həʊmwɜ:k]
devoirs 70
honey ['hʌnɪ] miel 39
hope [həʊp] espérer 27
horrible ['hɒrɪbl] horrible 64
horse [hɔ:s] cheval 95
hospital ['hɒspɪtl] hôpital 22
hot [hɒt] très chaud,
trop chaud 99
   be ~ avoir (trop) chaud 21

hotel [həʊ'tel] hôtel 82
hour ['aʊə] heure 13
house [haʊs] maison 47
how [haʊ] comment 33
How are you ?
Comment ça va ? 6
how many [haʊ 'menɪ]
combien 114
how much [haʊ mʌtʃ]
combien 111
hundred ['hʌndrɪd] cent 10
hungry ['hʌŋgrɪ] **(be ~)**
avoir faim 39
hurry ['hʌrɪ] se dépêcher 102
hurt [hɜ:t]**, hurt, hurt**
faire mal ; se faire mal 22
husband ['hʌzbənd] mari 17
hutch [hʌtʃ] clapier 95

I

I [aɪ] je
I am fed up J'en ai assez 61
ice [aɪs] glace 89
ice cream [aɪs kri:m] glace,
crème glacée 42
ice-skate [aɪs skeɪt] patiner 89
ice-skating [aɪs 'skeɪtɪŋ]
patinage 73
idea [aɪ'dɪə] idée 30
I don't care Ça m'est égal 61
if [ɪf] si 8
ill [ɪl] malade 22
in [ɪn] dans 108
insect ['ɪnsekt] insecte 93
inside ['ɪn'saɪd] dedans 107
intelligent [ɪn'telɪdʒənt]
intelligent 64

interesting ['ɪntrɪstɪŋ]
intéressant 62
into ['ɪntʊ] dans (direction) 8
invite [ɪn'vaɪt] inviter 75
island [aɪlənd] île 90
it [ɪt] il, elle (chose),
le, la, lui 112
It doesn't matter
Ça ne fait rien,
ce n'est pas grave 61
its [ɪts] son, sa, ses 112

J

jacket ['dʒækɪt] blouson 36
jam [dʒæm] confiture 39
January ['dʒænjʊərɪ] janvier 13
jeans [dʒi:nz] jeans 37
jewel ['dʒu:əl] bijou 54
job [dʒɒb] métier 78
judo ['dʒu:dəʊ] judo 73
juice [dʒu:s] jus 43
July [dʒu:'laɪ] juillet 13
jump [dʒʌmp] sauter 24
jumper ['dʒʌmpə] pull 37
June [dʒu:n] juin 13

K

kangaroo [ˌkæŋgə'ru:]
kangourou 96
keep [ki:p]**, kept, kept**
garder 57
key [ki:] clé 47
kind [kaɪnd] gentil 27
kiss [kɪs] embrasser 60
kitchen ['kɪtʃɪn] cuisine 52
knee [ni:] genou 18

knickers ['nɪkəz] culotte 36
knife/knives [naɪf] couteau 52
know [nəʊ], **knew, known**
connaître, savoir 30

L

ladder ['lædə] échelle 53
lamp [læmp] lampe 49
last [lɑːst] dernier 105, 109
late [leɪt] tard ; en retard 105
laugh [lɑːf] rire 27
lawn [lɔːn] pelouse 53
lazy ['leɪzɪ] paresseux 27
leaf/leaves [liːf] feuille 93
learn [lɜːn], **learnt, learnt**
apprendre 69
leave [liːv], **left, left**
partir (de), quitter 24
  Leave me alone
  Laisse-moi tranquille 61
leek [liːk] poireau 44
left [left] à gauche 108
leg [leg] jambe 18
lemon ['lemən] citron 45
less [les] moins 110
lesson ['lesn] cours, leçon 69
let's [lets] 117
letter ['letə] lettre 55
lettuce ['letɪs] laitue 44
library ['laɪbrərɪ] bibliothèque 82
lie [laɪ], **lay, lain** être allongé 24
lie [laɪ] mensonge ; mentir 31
lift [lift] ascenseur 46
light [laɪt] lumière 49 ; clair
66 ; léger 66
like [laɪk] comme 8 ; aimer,
bien aimer 26

lion ['laɪən] lion 117
lip [lɪp] lèvre 18
listen ['lɪsn] écouter 20, 23
little ['lɪtl] petit 65
  a little un peu (de) 110
live [lɪv] vivre, habiter 47
locomotive [ləʊkə'məʊtɪv]
locomotive 87
long [lɒŋ] long 19, 67
look [lʊk] regarder 20
look after [lʊk 'ɑːftə]
s'occuper de 60
look for [lʊk fɔː] chercher 59
lose [luːz], **lost, lost** perdre 72
a lot beaucoup 110
love [lʌv] aimer 26
lovely ['lʌvlɪ] charmant,
agréable ; joli 64
low [ləʊ] bas 65
luck [lʌk] chance 61
luggage ['lʌgɪdʒ] bagages 88
lunch [lʌntʃ] déjeuner 34, 38

M

make [meɪk], **made, made**
faire, fabriquer 58
man [mæn] homme 14
many ['menɪ] beaucoup de 114
map [mæp] plan, carte 88
marble ['mɑːbl] bille 75
March [mɑːtʃ] mars 13
market ['mɑːkɪt] marché 82
match [mætʃ] allumette 54 ;
match 72
matter ['mætə]
  What is the matter ?
  It doesn't matter 61

May [meɪ] mai 13
me [miː] me, moi 112
meal [miːl] repas 38
measure ['meʒə] mesurer 23
meat [miːt] viande 41
medicine ['medsɪn]
médicament 22
meet [miːt], **met, met**
rencontrer 60
middle ['mɪdl] milieu 109
midnight ['mɪdnaɪt] midnight 12
milk [mɪlk] lait 39, 43
minute ['mɪnɪt] minute 13
miss [mɪs] manquer, rater 88
  I ~ him il me manque 28
mistake [mɪs'teɪk] erreur 30
mix [mɪks] mélanger 58
Monday ['mʌndɪ] lundi 13
money ['mʌnɪ] argent 80
monkey ['mʌŋkɪ] singe 96
month [mʌnθ] mois 12, 13
mood [muːd] humeur 28
moon [muːn] lune 100
more [mɔː] plus 110
morning ['mɔːnɪŋ] matin 103
mother ['mʌðə] mère 16
motorbike ['məʊtəbaɪk]
moto 84, 86
motorway ['məʊtəweɪ]
autoroute 84
mountain ['maʊntɪn]
montagne 89
mouse [maʊs] souris 95
mouth [maʊθ] bouche 18
move [muːv] bouger 24
Mr ['mɪstə] monsieur 6
Mrs ['mɪsɪz] madame 6
much [mʌtʃ] beaucoup 114

mum [mʌm] maman 17

mummy ['mʌmɪ] maman 17

museum [mju:'zɪəm]
musée 75

mushroom ['mʌʃrʊm]
champignon 93

music ['mju:zɪk] musique 77

musician [mju:'zɪʃn]
musicien 78

must [mʌst] devoir 118

my [maɪ] mon, ma, mes 112

N

nail [neɪl] ongle 18 ; clou 54

naked ['neɪkɪd] nu 37

name [neɪm] nom 14

near [nɪə] près 107

nearly ['nɪəlɪ] presque 111

neck [nek] cou 18

need [ni:d] avoir besoin de 58

neighbour ['neɪbə] voisin 47

net [net] épuisette 91

never ['nevə] jamais 104

new [nju:] neuf, nouveau 66

newspaper ['nju:zpeɪpə]
journal 49

New Year [nju: jɪə]
le Nouvel An 101

next [nekst] prochain 102, 105

next to à côté de 106

nice [naɪs] sympathique,
gentil ; joli ; bon 64

night [naɪt] nuit 103

nightdress ['naɪtdres]
chemise de nuit 36

nine [naɪn] neuf 10

nineteen [naɪn'ti:n] dix-neuf 10

ninety ['naɪntɪ] quatre-vingt-
dix 10

no [nəʊ] non 9

no... [nəʊ] pas de 110, 114

noise [nɔɪz] bruit 20

noisy ['nɔɪzɪ] bruyant 20

nose [nəʊz] nez 18

not [nɒt] ne pas 8

note [nəʊt] billet de banque 80

nothing ['nʌðɪŋ] rien

November [nəʊ'vembə]
novembre 13

now [naʊ] maintenant 102

nowhere ['nəʊwɛə] nulle
part 107

number ['nʌmbə] chiffre 10

nurse [nɜ:s] infirmière 79

O

o'clock [ə'klɒk] heure

October [ɒk'təʊbə] octobre 13

off [ɒf] éteint 65

office ['ɒfɪs] bureau 82

often ['ɒfən] souvent 102

old [əʊld] vieux, âge 15, 66

on [ɒn] sur 107 ; allumé 65

one [wʌn] un, une 10

only ['əʊnlɪ] seulement 9

open ['əʊpən] ouvrir 58

opinion [ə'pɪnjən] avis 62

opposite ['ɒpəzɪt]
contraire 65

or [ɔ:] ou 9

orange ['ɒrɪndʒ] (couleur)
orange 11 ; (fruit) orange 45

ostrich ['ɒstrɪtʃ] autruche 97

ouch [aʊtʃ] aïe 20

our ['aʊə] notre, nos 112

out [aʊt] dehors,
vers l'extérieur 108

outside [,aʊt'saɪd] dehors 107

oven ['ʌvn] four 52

over ['əʊvə] fini, terminé 35 ;
par-dessus 106

owl [aʊl] hibou, chouette 93

P

paint [peɪnt] peindre 70

paintbrush ['peɪntbrʌʃ]
pinceau 70

paper ['peɪpə] papier 70

parent ['pɛərənt] parent 16

park [pɑ:k] parc, square 82

parrot ['pærət] perroquet 96

party ['pɑ:tɪ] fête 101

passenger ['pæsndʒə]
passager 86

pasta ['pæstə] pâtes 41

pavement ['peɪvmənt]
trottoir 83

pay [peɪ], **paid, paid** payer 80

peas [pi:z] petits pois 44

pear [pɛə] poire 45

pedal [pedl] pédale 86

pen [pen] stylo 70

pencil ['pensl] crayon 70

pencil case ['pensl keɪs]
trousse 71

penguin ['peŋgwɪn] pingouin 97

people ['pi:pl] gens 14

pepper ['pepə] poivre 40

perhaps [pə'hæps] peut-être 9

person ['pɜ:sn] personne 15

pet [pet] animal familier 53

photo [ˈfəʊtəʊ], **photograph** [ˈfəʊtəɡræf] photo 54

piano [ˈpjɑːnəʊ] piano 77

picnic [ˈpɪknɪk] pique-nique 75

picture [ˈpɪktʃə] image 55

pie [paɪ] tarte 42

piece [piːs] morceau 111

pig [pɪɡ] cochon 95

pigsty [ˈpɪɡstaɪ] porcherie 95

pillow [ˈpɪləʊ] oreiller 50

pineapple [ˈpaɪnˌæpl] ananas 45

pink [pɪŋk] rose (couleur) 11

pizza [ˈpiːtsə] pizza 41

place [pleɪs] place 106

plane [pleɪn] avion 87

plate [pleɪt] assiette 52

play [pleɪ] jouer 70

playground [ˈpleɪɡraʊnd] cour de récréation 70

playtime [ˈpleɪtaɪm] récréation 70

pleasant [ˈpleznt] agréable 63

please [pliːz] s'il te plaît, s'il vous plaît 6

pleased [pliːzd] content 28

plum [plʌm] prune 45

plumber [ˈplʌmə] plombier 78

pole vaulting [ˈpəʊl vɔːltɪŋ] saut à la perche 73

police station [pəˈliːs ˌsteɪʃn] commissariat 83

policeman [pəˈliːsmən] policier 78, 84

polite [pəˈlaɪt] poli 29

porthole [ˈpɔːthəʊl] hublot (de bateau) 87

postcard [ˈpəʊstkɑːd] carte postale 55

postman [ˈpəʊstmən] facteur 79

post office [ˈpəʊst ˌɔfɪs] poste 83

potato [pəˈteɪtəʊ] pomme de terre 44

pour [pɔː] verser 58

prefer [prɪˈfɜː] préférer 28

pregnant [ˈpreɡnənt] enceinte 17

present [ˈpreznt] cadeau 101

pretty [ˈprɪti] joli 64

price [praɪs] prix 80

problem [ˈprɒbləm] problème 30

pull [pʊl] tirer 58

pupil [ˈpjuːpl] élève 69

puppet [ˈpʌpɪt] marionnette 75

purple [ˈpɜːpl] violet 11

purse [pɜːs] porte-monnaie 80

push [pʊʃ] pousser 58

put [pʊt], **put, put** mettre 57

put down [pʊt daʊn] poser 57

put on [pʊt ɒn] mettre, enfiler (vêtement) 37

pyjamas [pɪˈdʒɑːməz] pyjama 37

Q

question [ˈkwestʃən] question 32

quick [kwɪk] rapide 105

quickly [ˈkwɪkli] vite, rapidement 105

quiet [ˈkwaɪət] calme, tranquille 28

quilt [kwɪlt] couette 50

R

rabbit [ˈræbɪt] lapin 95

race [reɪs] course 72

radio [ˈreɪdɪəʊ] radio 49

rain [reɪn] pleuvoir 98 ; pluie 99

rainbow [ˈreɪnbəʊ] arc-en-ciel 99

raincoat [ˈreɪnkəʊt] imperméable 36

read [riːd], **read, read** lire 71

ready [ˈredɪ] prêt 102

receive [rɪˈsiːv] recevoir 58

receptionist [rɪˈsepʃənɪst] réceptionniste 78

rectangle [ˈrekˌtæŋgl] rectangle 11

red [red] rouge 11

remember [rɪˈmembə] se rappeler, se souvenir de 30

repair [rɪˈpeə] réparer 59

reporter [rɪˈpɔːtə] journaliste, reporter 78

rest [rest] reste 111

restaurant [ˈrestərɔ̃ːŋ] restaurant 83

rice [raɪs] riz 41

ride [raɪd], **rode, ridden** monter à, faire du (cheval, vélo, moto) 85

right [raɪt] exact, juste, bon 68 ; à droite 108

ring [rɪŋ], **rang, rung** sonner 50

ring [rɪŋ] bague 55

river [ˈrɪvə] rivière 93

road [rəʊd] route 85

rock [rɒk] rocher 90

rollerblade [ˈrəʊləbleɪd] roller 75

roof [ruːf] toit 46
room [rʊm] pièce 46
rope [rəʊp] corde 55
round [raʊnd] rond 11
rubber ring [rʌbə rɪŋ] bouée 91
rude [ruːd] impoli 29
rugby ['rʌgbɪ] rugby 73
ruler [ruːlə] règle 71
run [rʌn], **ran, run** courir 24

S
sad [sæd] triste 28
saddle [sædl] selle 86
sailing boat ['seɪlɪŋ bəʊt]
voilier 90
salt [sɔːlt] sel 40
same [seɪm] pareil, même 66
sand [sænd] sable 90
sandcastle ['sændkɑːsl]
château de sable 90
sandwich ['sænwɪdʒ]
sandwich 41
Saturday ['sætədɪ] samedi 13
saucepan ['sɔːspæn]
casserole 52
sausage ['sɒsɪdʒ] saucisse 41
say [seɪ], **said, said** dire 32
scarf [skɑːf] foulard 36
scary ['skɛərɪ] effrayant 64
school [skuːl] école 68
schoolbag ['skʊːlbæg]
cartable 71
sea [siː] mer 90
seaside ['sɪːsaɪd] bord de mer 90
season ['siːzn] saison 99
second ['sekənd] deuxième,
second 109 ; seconde 13

secret ['siːkrɪt] secret 32
secretary ['sekrətrɪ]
secrétaire 78
see [siː], **saw, seen** voir 21
   See you soon À bientôt 6
   See you tomorrow
   À demain 6
sell [sel], **sold, sold** vendre 80
send [send], **sent, sent**
envoyer 59
sense [sens] sens 20
September [sep'tembə]
septembre 13
seven ['sevn] sept 10
seventeen [sevn'tiːn] dix-sept 10
seventy ['sevntɪ]
soixante-dix 10
sh, shh [ʃ] chut 20
shade [ʃeɪd] ombre 91
shake [ʃeɪk], **shook, shaken**
secouer 59
shampoo [ʃæm'puː]
shampooing 51
shape [ʃeɪp] forme 11
she [ʃiː] elle (personne) 112
sheep [ʃiːp] mouton 95
sheet [ʃiːt] drap 50
shell [ʃel] coquillage 91
shine [ʃaɪn], **shone, shone**
briller 99
ship [ʃɪp] navire 87
shirt [ʃɜːt] chemise 36
shoe [ʃuː] chaussure 36
shop [ʃɒp] magasin 81
shop assistant [ʃɒp ə'sɪstənt]
vendeur 81
shopkeeper ['ʃɒpkiːpə]
marchand, commerçant 81

shopping ['ʃɒpɪŋ] courses 81
short [ʃɔːt] court 19, 67
shoulder ['ʃəʊldə] épaule 18
shout [ʃaʊt] crier 32
show [ʃəʊ], **showed, shown**
montrer 71
show [ʃəʊ] spectacle 76
shower ['ʃaʊə] douche 51
shy [ʃaɪ] timide 28
sick [sɪk] : **feel ~**
avoir mal au cœur 22
sing [sɪŋ], **sang, sung**
chanter 77
sister ['sɪstə] sœur 16
sit [sɪt], **sat, sat** être assis 24
sit down [sɪt daʊn] s'asseoir 25
sitting room ['sɪtɪŋ rʊm]
salon 48
six [sɪks] six 10
sixteen [sɪks'tiːn] seize 10
sixty ['sɪkstɪ] soixante 10
ski [skiː] ski ; skier 89
ski pole [skiː pəʊl]
bâton de ski 89
skiing ['skɪːɪŋ] ski (sport) 73
skirt [skɜːt] jupe 36
sky [skaɪ] ciel 100
sled [sled] luge ;
faire de la luge 89
sleep [sliːp], **slept, slept**
dormir 35
slice [slaɪs] tranche 41
slow [sləʊ] lent 85, 105
small [smɔːl] petit 15
smell [smel], **smelt, smelt**
sentir 21
smile [smaɪl] sourire 29
snack [snæk] goûter 35

snow [snəʊ] neige 89 ; neiger 99

snowman ['snəʊmən]
bonhomme de neige 89

soap [səʊp] savon 51

sock [sɒk] chaussette 36

sofa ['səʊfə] canapé 49

soft [sɒft] doux, douce 21

some [sʌm] quelques 111

sometimes ['sʌmtaɪmz]
quelquefois 102

son [sʌn] fils 17

song [sɒŋ] chanson 77

soon [suːn] bientôt 102

sorry ['sɒrɪ] désolé, pardon 6

spaceship ['speɪsʃɪp]
navette spatiale 100

speak [spiːk], spoke, spoken
parler 32

spend [spend], spent, spent
dépenser 81

spinach ['spɪnɪdʒ] épinards 44

spoon [spuːn] cuiller 52

sport [spɔːt] sport 72

spring [sprɪŋ] printemps 99

square [skwɛə] carré 11

squeeze [skwiːz] presser 23

squirrel ['skwɪrəl] écureuil 93

stable [steɪbl] écuries 95

stairs [stɛəz] escalier 47

stamp [stæmp] timbre 55

stand up ['stænd ʌp], stood
up, stood up se lever 25

star [stɑː] étoile 100

start [stɑːt] commencer 105

station ['steɪʃən] gare 88

stay [steɪ] rester 25

steering wheel ['stɪərɪŋ wiːl]
volant 87

still [stɪl] encore, toujours 105

stop [stɒp] arrêt 84 ; arrêter 102

straight [streɪt] raide 19

straight on ['streɪt ɒn] tout
droit 108

strange [streɪndʒ] bizarre 64

strawberry ['strɔːbərɪ] fraise 45

street [striːt] rue 83

strict [strɪkt] sévère 29

strong [strɒŋ] fort 15

stupid ['stjuːpɪd] stupide 29

suburbs ['sʌbɜːbz] banlieue 83

sugar ['ʃʊgə] sucre 42

suitcase ['suːtkeɪs] valise 88

summer ['sʌmə] été 99

sun [sʌn] soleil 100

Sunday ['sʌndɪ] dimanche 13

sunglasses ['sʌnglɑːsɪz]
lunettes de soleil 89, 91

supermarket ['suːpəmɑːkɪt]
supermarché 81

sure [ʃʊə] sûr 31

surprised [sə'praɪzd] étonné 29

swallow ['swɒləʊ] avaler 23

sweet [swiːt] bonbon 42

swim [swɪm], swam, swum
nager 91

swimming ['swɪmɪŋ]
natation 73

swimming pool ['swɪmɪŋ
puːl] piscine 72

swimsuit ['swɪmsuːt]
maillot de bain 91

swing [swɪŋ] balançoire 53

switch off ['swɪtʃ ɒf]
éteindre 50

switch on ['swɪtʃ ɒn]
allumer 50

T

table ['teɪbl] table 52

take [teɪk], took, taken
prendre 59

take off ['teɪk ɒf] enlever
(vêtement) 37

talk [tɔːk] parler, discuter 32

tall [tɔːl] grand 15

taste [teɪst] goûter ; goût 21

taxi ['tæksɪ] taxi 85

tea [tiː] thé 39, 43

teach [tiːtʃ] enseigner,
apprendre (à quelqu'un) 71

teacher ['tiːtʃə] maître,
maîtresse, professeur 69, 78

team [tiːm] équipe 72

telephone ['telɪfəʊn]
téléphone 49

television ['telɪˌvɪʒən]
télévision 49

tell [tel], told, told dire,
raconter 33

tell off ['tel ɒf] gronder 33

temper ['tempə] caractère 29

ten [ten] dix 10

tennis ['tenɪs] tennis 73

thank you [θæŋk juː] merci 7

that [ðæt] ce, cette, cela 113

the [ðə] le, la, les 113

theatre ['θɪətə] théâtre 76

their [ðɛə] leur, leurs 112

them [ðem] les, eux, leur 112

then [ðen] ensuite 103

there [ðɛə] là, là-bas 106

there is/there are il y a 61

these [ðiːz] ces ...-ci, ceux-ci
113

they [ðeɪ] ils, elles 112

thick [θɪk] épais 67

thigh [θaɪ] cuisse 18

thin [θɪn] mince, maigre 15

thing [θɪŋ] chose, objet 54

think [θɪŋk]**, thought, thought** penser 30

third [θɜːd] troisième 109

thirsty ['θɜːstɪ] **: be ~** avoir soif 38

thirteen [θɜː'tiːn] treize 10

thirty ['θɜːtɪ] trente 10

this [ðɪs] ce ...-ci, cette ... -ci, ceci 113

this is... voici 7

those [ðəʊz] ces ... - là, ceux-là 113

thousand ['θaʊzənd] mille 10

three [θriː] trois 10

through [θruː] à travers 106

throw [θrəʊ]**, threw, thrown** lancer 59

thrown [θrəʊn] → **throw**

thumb [θʌm] pouce 36

thunderstorm ['θʌndəstɔːm] orage 98

Thursday ['θɜːzdɪ] jeudi 13

ticket ['tɪkɪt] billet, ticket 88

tiger ['taɪgə] tigre 97

tights [taɪtz] collant 36

time [taɪm] temps, heure 12, 102

timetable ['taɪmteɪbl] emploi du temps 12

tiny ['taɪnɪ] minuscule 67

tired ['taɪəd] fatigué 35

to [tuː] à 9

today [tə'deɪ] aujourd'hui 104

toe [təʊ] orteil 18

toilet ['tɔɪlɪt] toilettes 51

tomato [tə'mɑːtəʊ] tomate 44

tomorrow [tə'mɒrəʊ] demain 104

tongue [tʌŋ] langue 19

tonight [tə'naɪt] ce soir 103

too [tuː] trop 111

  too many [tuː 'menɪ] trop de 111

  too much [tuː mʌtʃ] trop de 111

tool [tuːl] outil 55

tooth/teeth [tuːθ] dent(s) 19

toothbrush ['tuːθbrʌʃ] brosse à dents 51

toothpaste ['tuːθpeɪst] dentifrice 51

top [tɒp] sommet 108

tortoise ['tɔːtəs] tortue 53

touch [tʌtʃ] toucher 21

towel ['taʊəl] serviette 51

town [taʊn] ville 82, 83

town hall ['taʊn hɔːl] mairie 83

toy [tɔɪ] jouet 76

tractor ['træktə] tracteur 95

traffic ['træfɪk] circulation 85

traffic jam ['træfɪk dʒæm] embouteillage 85

train [treɪn] train 86

trainers ['treɪnəz] baskets 37

transport ['trænspɔːt] transport 86

travel ['trævl] voyager 88

tree [triː] arbre 93

triangle ['traɪæŋgl] triangle 11

trousers ['traʊzəz] pantalon 36, 89

true [truː] vrai 31

trumpet ['trʌmpɪt] trompette 77

try [traɪ] essayer 59

T-shirt ['tɪʃɜːt] tee-shirt 36

tube [tjuːb] métro 85

Tuesday ['tjuːzdɪ] mardi 13

tummy ['tʌmɪ] ventre 18

turn [tɜːn] tour 109

TV ['tiːviː] télévision 49

twelve [twelv] douze 10

twenty ['twentɪ] vingt 10

two [tuː] deux 10

U

ugly ['ʌglɪ] laid 66

umbrella [ʌm'brelə] parapluie 99

uncle ['ʌŋkl] oncle 16

under ['ʌndə] sous 107

underground ['ʌndəgraʊnd] métro 85

understand [ˌʌndə'stænd]**, understood, understood** comprendre 30

unfair [ʌn'feə] injuste 63

unhappy [ʌn'hæpɪ] malheureux 28

universe ['juːnɪvɜːs] univers 100

unpleasant [ʌn'pleznt] désagréable 63

up [ʌp] en haut, vers le haut 108

upstairs ['ʌpsteəz] en haut (des escaliers), à l'étage 47

us [ʌs] nous

use [juːz] utiliser, se servir de 59

useful ['juːsfʊl] utile 8

usually ['juːʒʊəlɪ] d'habitude 105

V

van [væn] camionnette 86

VCR ['viː siː ɑː]
magnétoscope 49

vegetable ['vedʒɪtəbl]
légume 44

very ['verɪ] très 9

video ['vɪdɪəʊ] vidéo 49

video game ['vɪdɪəʊ geim]
jeu vidéo 76

village ['vɪlɪdʒ] village 93

violin [ˌvaɪə'lɪn] violon 77

visit ['vɪzɪt] visiter 76

W

wait (for) [weɪt] attendre 103

waiter [weɪtə] serveur 79

wake up [weɪk ʌp], **woke,
woken** se réveiller 34

walk [wɔːk] promenade 25 ;
marcher 25

wall [wɔːl] mur 47

want [wɒnt] vouloir 29

warm [wɔːm] tiède, chaud 99
 be ~ avoir (bien) chaud 21

wash [wɒʃ] laver ; se laver 51

watch [wɒtʃ] observer,
regarder 21 ; montre 12

water ['wɔːtə] eau 43

wave [weiv] vague 91

way [weɪ] direction 108

we [wiː] nous 112

wear [wɛə], **wore, worn**
porter (vêtement) 37

weather ['weðə] temps
(qu'il fait) 98

wedding ['wedɪŋ] mariage 101

Wednesday ['wenzdeɪ]
mercredi 13

week [wiːk] semaine 13

weekend ['wiːkend]
week-end 12

weigh [weɪ] peser 23

welcome ['welkəm]
bienvenue 7

well [wel] bien 71

wet [wet] mouillé 65

what [wɒt] que, quoi 33
 What is the matter ?
 Que se passe-t-il ? 61

wheel [wiːl] roue 85, 86

when [wen] quand 33, 103

where [wɛə] où 33, 106

white [waɪt] blanc, blanche 11

who [huː] qui 33

why [waɪ] pourquoi 33

wife [waɪf] femme, épouse 17

win [wɪn], **won, won** gagner 72

wind [wɪnd] vent 98

window ['wɪndəʊ] fenêtre 46

windscreen [wɪndskriːn]
pare-brise 86

wine [waɪn] vin 43

wing [wɪŋ] aile 87

winner ['wɪnə] gagnant,
vainqueur 72

winter ['wɪntə] hiver 89, 99

with [wɪð] avec 9

without [wɪð'aʊt] sans 9

wolf [wʊlf] loup 97

woman ['wʊmən] femme 15

wonder ['wʌndə]
se demander 30

wonderful ['wʌndəfʊl]
merveilleux 64

wood [wʊd] bois 93

word [wɜːd] mot 8, 33

work [wɜːk] travailler 70 ;
fonctionner, marcher 55

world [wɜːld] monde 100

worry ['wʌrɪ] s'inquiéter 29

worse [wɜːs] pire 63

worst [wɜːst] le pire, la pire 63

wrist [rɪst] poignet 18

write [raɪt], **wrote, written**
écrire 71

wrong [rɒŋ] faux 68

Y

year [jɪə] année 13, 105

yellow ['jeləʊ] jaune 11

yes [jes] oui 9

yesterday ['jestədeɪ] hier 104

yoghurt ['jəʊgət] yaourt 42

you [juː] tu, te, toi, vous 112

young [jʌŋ] jeune 15

your [jɔː] ton, ta, tes, votre, vos
112

Z

zebra ['ziːbrə] zèbre 97

zero ['zɪərəʊ] zéro 10

zoo [zuː] zoo 96

INDEX
FRANÇAIS-ANGLAIS

A

à bientôt see you soon 6
à demain
see you tomorrow 6
à at 106 ; to 9
accident accident 84
accrocher hang up, hung,
hung 57
acheter buy, bought, bought
80
acteur actor 76
action action 56
actrice actress 76
adresse address 47
adulte adult 14
aéroport airport 88
âge years old 15
Quel âge as-tu ?
How old are you ? 15
agité excited 27
agréable pleasant 63
aider help 60
aïe ouch 20
aigle eagle 96
aile wing 87
aimer (bien) like 26
aimer, adorer love 26
aller go, went, gone 24, 34
allongé (être) lie, lay, lain 24
allumé on 65
allumer switch on 50
allumette match 54
alphabet alphabet 68

amener bring, brought,
brought 56
ami friend 69
amusant funny 62
s'amuser have fun 35
ananas pineapple 45
an year 13, 105
Nouvel An New Year 101
âne donkey 94
animal animal 92
animal familier pet 53
année year 13, 105
anniversaire birthday 101
anorak anorak 89
août August 13
appareil photo camera 74
appartement flat 47
appeler call 32
apporter bring, brought,
brought 56
apprendre learn, learnt,
learnt 69 ;
    (à quelqu'un à faire
quelque chose) teach 71
après after 104
après-midi afternoon 7, 103
    bon après-midi
    good afternoon 7
arbre tree 93
arc-en-ciel rainbow 99
architecte architect 78
argent money 80
armoire cupboard 52
arrêt de bus bus stop 84
arrêter stop 102
ascenseur lift 46
s'asseoir sit down, sat, sat 25
assez enough 110

J'en ai assez I am fed up 61
assiette plate 52
assis (être) sit, sat, sat 24
astronaute astronaut 100
atchoum atishoo 20
attendre wait (for) 103
attention (faire) be careful
61
attraper catch, caught,
caught 56
au revoir goodbye, bye-bye,
bye 7
aujourd'hui today 104
autobus bus 84
automne autumn 99
autoroute motorway 84
autour around 106
autruche ostrich 97
avaler swallow 23
avant before 104
avec with 9
avion plane 87
avis opinion 62
avoir have, had, had 57
avril April 13

B

bacon bacon 41
bagages luggage 88
se bagarrer fight, fought,
fought 69
bague ring 55
baignoire bath 51
bain bath 35, 51
balançoire swing 53
ballon ball 74
banane banana 45
bande dessinée comics 74

banlieue suburbs 83

banque bank 82

banquier banker 78

bas, basse low 65

en bas down 108 ;
   (des escaliers)
   downstairs 47

basket basketball 73 ;
   (chaussures) trainers 37

basse-cour farmyard 95

bateau boat 87 ;
   (gros bateau) ship 87

bâtiment building 82

bâton stick 89

bâton de ski ski pole 89

se battre fight, fought, fought
69

beau, belle beautiful 66

beaucoup a lot of 110 ;
many ; much 114

bébé baby 14

besoin (avoir ~ de) need 58

beurre butter 39

bibliothèque library 82

bien sûr of course 31, 61

bien good 62 ; well 71

bientôt soon 102

bienvenue welcome 7

bijou jewel 54

bille marble 75

billet ticket 88 ;
   (de banque) note 80

biscuit biscuit 42

blanc white 11

bleu blue 11

blouson jacket 36

bœuf beef 40

boire drink, drank, drunk 38

bois wood 93

boisson drink 43

boîte box/boxes 54

bon après-midi
good afternoon 7

bon good 62 ; nice 64 ;
   (exact) right 68

bonbon sweet 42

bonhomme de neige
snowman 89

bonjour hello 7 ;
   (le matin) good morning 7;
   (l'après-midi)
   good afternoon 7

bonne affaire bargain 80

bonne chance good luck 61

bonne nuit goodnight 7

bonsoir good evening 7

bord de mer seaside 90

botte boot 36

bouche mouth 18

boucher butcher 79

bouclé curly 19

bouée rubber ring 91

bouger move 24

boulanger baker 78

bouteille bottle 52

boxe boxing 73

bras arm 18

briller shine, shone, shone 99

brosse à cheveux hairbrush 51

brosse à dents toothbrush 51

bruit noise 20

brûlant hot 99

bruyant noisy 20

bureau (meuble) desk 68 ;
   (pièce) office 82

bus bus 84

C

Ça m'est égal
I don't care 61

Ça ne fait rien
It doesn't matter 61

cabine cabin 87

cache-cache hide-and-seek
75

cadeau present 101

café (boisson) coffee 43 ;
   (lieu) café 82

cahier exercise book 71

calme quiet 28

cameraman cameraman 78

camionnette van 86

campagne country 92

canapé sofa 49

canard duck 94

capitale capital 83

capot bonnet 86

caractère temper 29

carotte carrot 44

carré square 11

cartable schoolbag 71

carte card 74 ;
   (géo.) map 88

carte postale postcard 55

casque helmet 84

casquette cap 36

casser break, broke, broken 56

casserole saucepan 52

cave cellar 46

CD CD 77

Ce n'est pas grave
It doesn't matter 61

ce this, that 113

ceci this 113

ceinture belt 36

cela that 113
cent hundred 10
cercle circle 11
céréales cereal 39
cerise cherry 45
ces these, those 113
   ces ...-ci these 113
   ces ... - là those 113
cette this, that 113
ceux-ci these 113
ceux-là those 113
chaise chair 52
chambre bedroom 50
chameau camel 96
champ field 94
champignon mushroom 93
champion champion 72
chance (bonne ~ !)
good luck ! 61
chanson song 77
chanter sing, sang, sung 77
chapeau hat 37
chaque every 110
charmant lovely 64
chat cat 53
château de sable sandcastle 90
chaud warm 21, 98 ; hot 21, 99
chaussette sock 36
chaussure shoe 36
cheminée
   (extérieure) chimney 46 ;
   (intérieure) fireplace 48 ;
   (de bateau) funnel 87
chemise shirt 36
chemise de nuit
nightdress 36

chemisier blouse 36
cher, chère
   (personne) dear 6 ;
   (prix) expensive 81
peu cher, peu chère cheap 81
chercher look for 59
chéri(e) darling 6
cheval horse 95
cheveux hair 18, 19
cheville ankle 18
chèvre goat 94
chez at 106
chien dog 53
chiffre number 10
chocolat chocolate 42
chocolat chaud cocoa, hot chocolate 43
chose thing 54
chou cabbage 44
chouette owl 93
chou-fleur cauliflower 44
chut sh 20
cidre cider 43
ciel sky 100
cinéma cinema 76
cinq five 10
cinquante fifty 10
circulation traffic 85
cirque circus 74
citron lemon 45
clair light 66
clapier hutch 95
classe (élèves) class 68 ;
   (salle) classroom 68
clé key 47
clou nail 54
cochon pig 95

coiffeur hairdresser 79
colère (en ~) angry 26
collant tights 36
colle glue 54
combien how many 111 ; how much 111
comme like 8
commencer begin, began, begun 109 ; start 105
comment how 33
Comment ça va ?
How are you ? 6
commerçant shopkeeper 81
commissariat police station 83
compétition competition 72
comprendre understand, understood, understood 30
compter count 68
concombre cucumber 44
conducteur driver 87
conduire drive, drove, driven 84
confiture jam 39
confortable comfortable 48
connaître know, knew, known 30
construire build, built, built 56
content pleased 28 ; glad 28
contraire opposite 65
copain friend 69
coq cock 94
coquillage shell 91
corde rope 55
corps body 18
côté (à ~ de) next to 106
cou neck 18
coude elbow 18

couette quilt 50
couleur colour 11
couper cut, cut, cut 56
cour de récréation playground 70
courageux, courageuse brave 26
courir run, ran, run 24
cours lesson 69
course race 72
courses shopping 81
court short 19
cousin, cousine cousin 16
coussin cushion 48
couteau knife/knives 52
coûter cost, cost, cost 80
couverture blanket 50
crabe crab 90
craie chalk 68
crayon pencil 70
crème (anglaise) custard 42
crier shout 32
crocodile crocodile 96
croire believe 31
cuiller spoon 52
cuire cook 38
cuisine (pièce) kitchen 52
cuisiner cook 38
cuisse thigh 18
culotte knickers 36

D
d'accord (être ~) agree 60
    ne pas être ~ disagree 60
dans in 108 ;
    (direction) into 8
danser dance 74

dauphin dolphin 96
de from 9
début beginning 109
décembre December 13
déçu disappointed 27
dedans inside 107
dégoûtant disgusting 64
se déguiser dress up 75
dehors outside 107 ;
    (vers l'extérieur) out 108
déjeuner lunch 34, 38
délicieux delicious 38
demain tomorrow 104
demander ask 32
se demander wonder 30
dent tooth/teeth 19
dentifrice toothpaste 51
dentiste dentist 22
se dépêcher hurry 102
dépenser spend, spent, spent 81
déranger disturb 60
dernier last 105, 109
derrière behind 107 ;
    (fesses) bottom 18
désagréable unpleasant 63
désolé sorry 6
dessin animé cartoon 76
dessin drawing 69
dessiner draw, drew, drawn 69
par dessus over 105
détester hate 26
deux two 10
deuxième second 109
devant in front of 107
devenir become, became, become 79
deviner guess 30
devoir must 118

devoirs homework 70
dictionnaire dictionary 69
différent different 66
difficile difficult 63
dimanche Sunday 13
dîner dinner 35, 38
dire say, said, said 32 ;
    (raconter) tell, told, told 33
direction way 108
discuter talk 32
se disputer argue 60
divorcé divorced 17
dix ten 10
dix-huit eighteen 10
dix-neuf nineteen 10
dix-sept seventeen 10
docteur doctor 22, 78
doigt finger 18
donner give, gave, given 57
dormir sleep, slept, slept 35
dos back 18
douche shower 51
doux, douce soft 21
douze twelve 10
drap sheet 50
droit (tout ~) straight on 108
droite (à ~) right 108
drôle funny 62
dur hard 20

E
eau water 43
échecs chess 74
échelle ladder 53
école school 68
écouter listen (to) 20, 23
écrire write, wrote, written 71

écureuil squirrel 93
écurie stable 95
effrayant scary 64
effrayé frightened 27
égal (ça m'est égal)
I don't care 61
église church 82
éléphant elephant 96
élève pupil 69
elle (personne) she ;
    (chose) it 112
elles they 112
embêter bother 60
embouteillage traffic jam 85
embrasser kiss 60
emploi du temps timetable 12
enceinte pregnant 17
encore (à nouveau) again
102
endormi asleep 35, 67
enfant child 14, 17
enfiler (vêtement) put on
37
enlever (vêtement)
take off 37
ennuyer bother 60
s'ennuyer be bored 26
ennuyeux, ennuyeuse
boring 62
énorme enormous 67
enseigner teach 71
ensuite then 103
entendre hear 20
s'entendre avec
get on with 60
entre between 106
entrer come in 25
enveloppe envelope 55

envoyer send, sent, sent 59
épais, épaisse thick 67
épaule shoulder 18
épicier grocer 79
épinards spinach 44
épuisette net 91
équipe team 72
erreur mistake 30
escalier stairs 47
escrime fencing 73
espérer hope 27
essayer try 59
et and 8
étable cowshed 95
été summer 99
éteindre switch off 50
éteint off 65
étoile star 100
étonné surprised 29
être be 116
exact right 68
examiner examine 23
excité excited 27
excuse-moi, excusez-moi
excuse me 6
expression expression 61

F
fabriquer make, made, made
58
facile easy 63
facteur postman 79
faim (avoir ~) be hungry
39, 116
faire do, did, did 56 ;
    (fabriquer) make, made,
    made 58

famille family 16
fantastique fantastic 62
farine flour 40
fatigué tired 35
fauteuil armchair 48
faux, fausse wrong 68
femme woman 15 ;
    (de quelqu'un) wife 17
fenêtre window 46
ferme farm 94, 95
fermer close 58
fermier farmer 78, 94
fesses bottom 18
fête party 101
fêter celebrate 101
feu d'artifice fireworks 101
feu fire 48
feuille leaf/leaves 93
février February 13
fille girl 14 ;
    (de quelqu'un) daughter 17
film film 76
fils son 17
fin end 109
finir finish 105
fleur flower 92
fonctionner work 55
fond bottom 108
football football 73
forêt forest 92
forme shape 11
fort strong 15
foulard scarf 36
four oven 52
fourchette fork 52
frais, fraîche cool 99
fraise strawberry 45
frère brother 16

frites chips 40
froid cold 21 ; 99
fromage cheese 40
front forehead 18
fruit fruit 45

G

gagnant winner 72
gagner win, won, won 72
gant glove 89
garage garage 53
garçon boy 14
garder keep, kept, kept 57
gare station 88
gâteau cake 42
gauche (à ~) left 108
génial great 62
genou knee 18
gens people 14
gentil kind 27 ; nice 64
gilet cardigan 36
girafe giraffe 96
glace ice 89 ;
  (dessert) ice cream 42
gomme eraser 71
goût taste 21
goûter taste 21 ;
  (repas) snack 35
grand tall 15 ; big 65
grand-mère grandmother 16
grand-parents grandparents
16
grand-père grandfather 16
grange barn 94
gratuit free 81
grenier attic 46
grenouille frog 92

grimper climb 24
gris grey 11
gronder tell off 33
gros, grosse fat 14
groupe (musique) band 77
guidon handlebars 86
guitare guitar 77
gymnastique gymnastics 73

H

habillé dressed 37
s'habiller get dressed 35, 37
d'habitude usually 105
habiter live 47
Halloween Hallowe'en 101
hamburger hamburger 41
hanche hip 18
haricot bean 44
haut high 65
  en ~ up 108 ;
  (des escaliers) upstairs 47
herbe grass 92
heure hour 13 ; time 12, 102
  Il est 5 heures
  It's 5 o'clock
heureux happy 28
hi hi ha ha 20
hibou owl 93
hier yesterday 104
hiver winter 89, 99
hobby hobby 74
homme man/men 14
honte (avoir ~) be ashamed
26
hôpital hospital 22
horrible horrible 64
hôtel hotel 82

huit eight 10
humeur mood 28

I

ici here 106
idée idea 30
il (personne) he ;
  (chose) it 112
il y a there is/there are 61
île island 90
ils they 112
image picture 55
immeuble building 82
imperméable raincoat 36
impoli rude 29
infirmière nurse 79
informaticien
computer technician 78
ingénieur engineer 78
injuste unfair 63
s'inquiéter worry 29
insecte insect 93
intelligent intelligent 64
intéressant interesting 62
inviter invite 75

J

jamais never 104
jambe leg 18
jambon ham 40
janvier January 13
jardin garden 53
jaune yellow 11
je I (pronom) 112
jeans jeans 37
jeu game 75

jeu vidéo video game 76

jeudi Thursday 13

jeune young 15

joli lovely 64 ; nice 64 ;
pretty 64

joue cheek 18

jouer play 70

jouet toy 76

jour day 12, 34, 103

journal newspaper 49

journaliste journalist,
reporter 78

journée day 34

judo judo 73

juillet July 13

juin June 13

jupe skirt 36

jus juice 43

juste fair 63

K

kangourou kangaroo 69

L

la the 113

la, à elle (personne) her ;
 (chose) it 113

là, là-bas there 106

laid ugly 66

laisser (~ tomber) drop 56
 Laisse-moi tranquille
 Leave me alone 61

lait milk 39, 43

laitue lettuce 44

lampe lamp 49

lancer throw, threw, thrown 59

langue tongue 19

lapin rabbit 95

laver wash 51

se laver wash 51

le the 113

le, à lui (personne) him ;
 (chose) it 113

leçon lesson 69

léger light 66

légume vegetable 44

lent slow 85, 105

les the 113

les (à eux, à elles) them 112

lettre letter 55

leur (à eux, à elles) them 112

leur, leurs their 112

se lever stand up, stood,
stood 25 ; (du lit) get up 34

lèvre lip 18

lion lion 97

lire read, read, read 71

lit bed 50

livre book 71

locomotive engine,
locomotive 87

loin far 107

loisir hobby 74

long long 19

losange diamond 11

loup wolf/wolves 97

lourd heavy 66

luge sled, sledge 89

faire de la luge sled, sledge
89

lui (à lui) him ; (à elle) her ;
 (chose) it 112

lumière light 49

lundi Monday 13

lune moon 100

lunettes de soleil
sunglasses 91

M

ma my 112

maçon builder 78

madame Mrs 6

magasin shop 81

magnétoscope VCR, video
cassette recorder 49

magnifique beautiful 66

mai May 13

maillot de bain swimsuit 91

main hand 18

maintenant now 102

mairie town hall 83

mais but 8

maison house 47

maison (à la ~) home 46

maître, maîtresse teacher
69, 78

mal (faire ~ ; se faire ~)
hurt, hurt, hurt 22
 avoir ~ au cœur feel sick 22

malade ill 22

malheureux unhappy 28

malin, maligne clever 26

maman mummy, mum 17

manger eat, ate, eaten 34, 38

manquer miss 88
 Il me manque I miss him 28

manteau coat 36

marchand shopkeeper 81

marché market 82

marcher walk 25 ;
 (machine) work 55

mardi Tuesday 13
mari husband 17
se marier get married 17
mariage wedding 101
marionnette puppet 75
marron brown 11
mars March 13
marteau hammer 54
masque de plongée
diving mask 91
match match 72
matin morning 103
mauvais bad 63
me me 112
médicament medicine 22
meilleur better 62
   le meilleur, la meilleure
   the best 62
mélanger mix 58
même even 8 ;
   (pareil) same 66
mensonge lie 31
mentir lie 31
menton chin 18
mer sea 90
merci thank you 7
mercredi Wednesday 13
mère mother 16
merveilleux wonderful 64
mes my 112
mesurer measure 23
métier job 78
métro tube, underground 85
mettre put, put, put 57 ;
   (un vêtement) put on 37
meubles furniture 46
miel honey 39
mieux better 62

le mieux the best 62
milieu middle 109
mille thousand 10
mince thin 15
minuit midnight 12
minuscule tiny 67
minute minute 13
moi me 112
moins less 110
mois month 12, 13
moitié half 110
mon my 112
monde world 100
monnaie change 80
monsieur Mr 6
montagne mountain 89
monter à (cheval, vélo,
moto) ride, rode, ridden 85
montre watch 12
montrer show, showed,
shown 71
morceau piece 111
mort dead 65
mot word 8, 33
moteur engine 84
moto motorbike 84, 86
mouillé wet 65
mouton sheep 95
mur wall 47
musée museum 75
musicien musician 78
musique music 77

N

nager swim, swam, swum 91
natation swimming 73
navette spatiale spaceship 100

navire ship 87
ne pas not 8
neige snow 89
neiger snow 99
neuf new 66
neuf (chiffre) nine 10
nez nose 18
Noël Christmas 101
noir black 11
nom name 14
non no 9
notre, nos our 112
nourriture food 40
nous (sujet) we ;
   (complément) us 112
nouveau new 66
   à ~ again 102
Nouvel An New Year 101
novembre November 13
nu naked 37
nuage cloud 98
nuit night 103
   bonne nuit goodnight 7
nulle part nowhere 107

O

objet thing 54
observer watch 21
obtenir get, got, gotten 57
occupé busy 35
s'occuper de look after 60
octobre October 13
œil eye 18
œuf egg 41
oiseau bird 92
ombre shade 91
oncle uncle 16

ongle nail 18
onze eleven 10
orage thunderstorm 98
orange (couleur) orange 11 ;
   (fruit) orange 45
ordinateur computer 54
oreille ear 18
oreiller pillow 50
orteil toe 18
ou or 9
où where 33, 106
oublier forget, forgot,
forgotten 30
oui yes 9
ours bear 97
outil tool 55
ouvrir open 58
ovale oval 11

P
pain bread 39
pantalon trousers 36
papa daddy, dad 17
papier paper 70
papillon butterfly 92
Pâques Easter 101
parapluie umbrella 99
parc park 82
parce que because 8
pardon excuse me 6 ; sorry 6
pare-brise windscreen 86
pare-chocs bumper 86
pareil same 66
parent parent 16
paresseux lazy 27
parler speak, spoke, spoken
32 ; talk 32

partir leave, left, left 24
partout everywhere 107
pas de no 110, 114
passager passenger 86
Que se passe-t-il ?
What's the matter ? 61
passionnant exciting 62
pâtes pasta 41
patiner (sur glace)
ice-skate 89
patinage ice-skating 73
payer pay, paid, paid 80
peau skin 18
pêche (poisson) fishing 87
pédale pedal 86
peindre paint 70
peintre painter 70
pelouse lawn 53
penser think, thought,
thought 30
perdre lose, lost, lost 72
père father 16
perroquet parrot 96
personne (quelqu'un)
person 15
peser weigh 23
petit déjeuner breakfast 38,
39
petit pois pea 44
petit little 65 ; small 15
un peu (un ~) a little 110
peur (avoir ~) be afraid 26
peut-être perhaps 9
phare (de véhicule)
headlight 86
pharmacien chemist 79
photo photo, photograph 54
piano piano 77

pièce room 46 ;
   (argent) coin 80
pied foot/feet 18
pinceau paintbrush 70
pingouin penguin 97
pique-nique picnic 75
pire worse 63
le pire, la pire the worst 63
piscine swimming pool 72
pizza pizza 41
placard cupboard 52
place place 106
plage beach 90
plan map 88
plancher floor 48
plat flat 67
plein full 66
pleurer cry 27
pleuvoir rain 98
plier fold 57
plombier plumber 78
pluie rain 99
plus more 110
poignet wrist 18
poire pear 45
poireau leek 44
poisson fish 40
poitrine chest 18
poivre pepper 40
poli polite 29
policier policeman 78, 84
pomme de terre potato 44
pomme apple 45
pompier fireman 79
porcherie pigsty 95
portail gate 53
porte door 46
porte-monnaie purse 80

porter carry 56 ;
  (un vêtement) wear, wore, worn 37
poser put down 57
poste post office 83
pouce thumb 36
poule hen 94
poulet chicken 40
poupée doll 74
pour for 8
pourquoi why 33
pousser push 58
pouvoir can 118
préféré favourite 64
préférer prefer 28
premier first 109
prendre take, took, taken 59
près near 107
presque nearly 111
presser squeeze 23
prêt ready 102
printemps spring 99
prix price 80
problème problem 30
prochain next 102, 105
professeur teacher 69, 78
profond deep 67
promenade walk 25
propre clean 65
prune plum 45
pull jumper 37
pyjama pyjamas 37

Q

quand when 33, 103
quarante forty 10
quatorze fourteen 10

quatre four 10
quatre-vingts eighty 10
quatre-vingt-dix ninety 10
que what 33
quelquefois sometimes 102
quelques some 111
question question 32
qui who 33
quinze fifteen 10
quitter leave, left, left 24
quoi what 33

R

raconter tell, told, told 33
radio radio 49
raide straight 19
raisin grapes 45
rapide fast 85 ; quick 105
rapidement quickly 105
se rappeler remember 30
rater miss 88
ravi glad 28
rayonnage bookshelf 48
réceptionniste receptionist 78
recevoir get, got, gotten 57
recevoir receive 58
récréation playtime 70
rectangle rectangle 11
réfrigérateur fridge 52
regarder look (at) 20 ;
  (observer) watch 21
remplir fill 56
renard fox 92
rencontrer meet, met, met 60
rendre give back 57
réparer repair 59
repas meal 38

répondre answer 32
réponse answer 32
reporter reporter 78
restaurant restaurant 83
reste rest 111
rester stay 25
retard (en ~) late 105
réveil alarm clock 12, 50
réveillé awake 67
se réveiller wake up, woke, woken 34
revenir come back 25
rhume cold 22
rideau curtain 48
rien nothing
  Ça ne fait rien
  It doesn't matter 61
rire laugh 27
rivière river 93
riz rice 41
robe dress 37
rocher rock 90
roller rollerblade 75
rond round 11
rose (couleur) pink 11
roue wheel 85, 86
rouge red 11
route road 85
rue street 83
rugby rugby 73

S

s'il te plaît, s'il vous plaît please 6
sa (à lui) his ; **(à elle)** her ; **(chose)** its 112
sable sand 90

sac bag 54

saison season 99

sale dirty 65

salle de bains bathroom 51

salon sitting room 48

salopette dungarees 36

salut hello 87

samedi Saturday 13

sandwich sandwich 41

sang blood 19

sans without 9

santé health 22
   en bonne ~ healthy 22

saucisse sausage 41

saut à la perche
pole vaulting 73

sauter jump 24

savoir know, knew, known 30

savon soap 51

sec, sèche dry 65

second second 109

seconde second 13

secouer shake, shook, shaken 59

secret secret 32

secrétaire secretary 78

seize sixteen 10

sel salt 40

selle saddle 86

semaine week 13

sens sense 20

sentiment feeling 26

sentir (odeur) smell, smelt, smelt 21 ; feel, felt, felt 23, 27
   se ~ feel, felt, felt 23, 27

sept seven 10

septembre September 13

serveur waiter 79

serviette towel 51

se servir de use 59

ses (à lui) his ; (à elle) her ; (chose) its 112

seulement only 9

sévère strict 29

shampooing shampoo 51

si if 8

singe monkey 96

six six 10

ski ski 89

skier ski 89

sœur sister 16

soif (avoir ~) be thirsty 38

soir evening 103
   ce ~ tonight 103

soixante sixty 10

soixante-dix seventy 10

sol floor 48

soleil sun 100

sombre dark 66

sommet top 108

son (à lui) his ; (à elle) her ; (chose) its 112

sonner ring, rang, rung 50

souffler blow, blew, blown 98

sourire smile 29

souris mouse 95

sous under 107

se souvenir de remember 30

souvent often 102

spectacle show 76

sport sport 72

square park 82

stupide stupid 29

sucre sugar 42

suivre follow 109

super great 62

supermarché supermarket 81

sur on 107

sûr sure 31

suspendre hang up, hung, hung 57

sympathique nice 64

T

ta your 112

table table 52

tableau noir blackboard 68

talon heel 18

tambour drum 77

tante aunt 16

tapis carpet 48

tard late 105

tarte pie 42

tasse cup 52

taxi taxi 85

te you 112

tee-shirt T-shirt 36

téléphone telephone 49

télévision television, TV 49

temps
   (qu'il fait) weather 98 ;
   (qui passe) time 102

tennis tennis 73 ;
   (chaussures) trainers 37

terminer finish 105

Terre Earth 100

tes your 112

tête head 18

thé tea 39, 43

théâtre theatre 76

ticket ticket 88

tiède (chaud) warm 21, 98

tigre tiger 97

timbre stamp 55
timide shy 28
tirer pull 58
tiroir drawer 48
toi you 112
toilettes toilet 51
toit roof 46
tomate tomato 44
tomber fall, fell, fallen 24
   laisser ~ drop 56
ton your 112
tortue tortoise 53
tôt early 105
toucher touch 21
toujours always 104
tour turn 109
tousser cough 23
tout, tous, toutes all 110 ;
every 110
tracteur tractor 95
train train 86
tranche slice 41
tranquille quiet 28
   Laisse-moi tranquille
   Leave me alone 61
transports transport 86
travailler work 70
à travers through 106
traverser cross 84
treize thirteen 10
trente thirty 10
très very 9
triangle triangle 11
triste sad 28
trois three 10
troisième third 109
trompette trumpet 77
trop too, too many (much) 111

trousse pencil case 71
trouver find, found, found 59
tu you 112
tuba snorkel 91

U
un, une a, an 112 ; one 10
univers universe 100
utile useful 8
utiliser use 59

V
vacances holiday 88
vache cow 94
vague wave 91
vainqueur winner 72
valise suitcase 88
vélo bicycle, bike 74, 86
vendeur shop assistant 81
vendre sell, sold, sold 80
vendredi Friday 13
venir come, came, come 25
vent wind 98
ventre tummy 18
vérifier test 23
verre glass 52
verser pour 58
vert green 11
vêtements clothes 36
viande meat 41
vide empty 66
vidéo video 49
   jeu ~ video game 76
vieux, vieille old 15, 66
village village 93
ville town 82, 83 ;

(grande) city 83
vin wine 43
vingt twenty 10
violet purple 11
violon violin 77
visage face 19
visiter visit 76
vite fast 85 ; quickly 105
vivant alive 65
vivre live 47
voici this is 7
voilier sailing boat 90
voir see, saw, seen 21
voisin neighbour 47
voiture car 86
volant wheel 86
voler fly, flew, flown 92
vos your 112
votre your 112
vouloir want 29
vous you 112
voyager travel 88
vrai true 31

W Y Z
week-end weekend 13
wagon carriage 86
yaourt yoghurt 42
zèbre zebra 97
zéro zero 10
zoo zoo 96